American Paintings,
Watercolors, and Drawings
from the Collection of
Rita and Daniel Fraad

American Paintings, Watercolors, and Drawings
from the Collection of
Rita and Daniel Fraad

LINDA AYRES *and* JANE MYERS

AMON CARTER MUSEUM 1985

© 1985 Amon Carter Museum of Western Art, Fort Worth, Texas
All rights reserved
Printed in the United States of America
International Standard Book Number 0-88360-075-7
Library of Congress Catalog Card Number 85-070941

This publication was produced in conjunction with an
exhibition held at the Amon Carter Museum from
May 24 to July 14, 1985.

Illustrated on cover: George Bellows, *Shore House*,
January 1911, oil on canvas, 40 × 42 in. (101.6 × 106.7 cm)
(cat. no. 45).

CONTENTS

FOREWORD
Jan Keene Muhlert
vii

ACKNOWLEDGMENTS
ix

INTRODUCTION
Linda Ayres
xi

CATALOGUE
Linda Ayres and Jane Myers
I

INDEX
109

FOREWORD

THE AMON CARTER MUSEUM is pleased to have the opportunity to present *American Paintings, Watercolors, and Drawings from the Collection of Rita and Daniel Fraad*. The fifty-one works lent by the Fraads, collected over the last thirty years, bring together an impressive group of American realist and impressionist art of the late nineteenth and early twentieth centuries. Their distinguished collection fortuitously complements the Amon Carter Museum's own holdings.

This publication honors the Fraads, who were pioneers not only in the collecting of American art but also in its conservation, research, and documentation. They have assiduously gathered from many sources material regarding the provenance, exhibition history, and other information on their paintings and works on paper, setting a high standard for other collectors. We thank them for generously sharing their files with us in preparation for the exhibition and catalogue. The Amon Carter Museum is deeply indebted to Rita and Daniel Fraad for their unfailing cooperation, for their support of all aspects of this project, and, especially, for lending us some of their many treasures.

We would also like to express our gratitude to Raymond and Margaret Horowitz, whose Prendergast watercolor *Picnicking Children—Central Park*, jointly owned with the Fraads, is in the exhibition. Margery Barbagallo, secretary to Daniel Fraad, cheerfully answered many questions and provided access to the object files and photographs. Arthur Vitols at Helga Photo Studio produced the color transparencies, and Marjorie Shelley and Joseph Griffin provided conservation expertise.

I am most grateful to Linda Ayres, curator of paintings and sculpture at the Amon Carter Museum, who conceived the idea for the exhibition and to Jane Myers, assistant curator, who worked with Linda to produce this beautiful exhibition and catalogue. They join me in extending appreciation to fellow staff members Ron Tyler, assistant director for collections and programs, for his supervision of the catalogue production and Milan Hughston, associate librarian, for his efficient assistance in answering reference questions and obtaining materials from other libraries. We also wish to acknowledge Palmer McCarter, Sidney Mass, and Trish Matthews, who typed the manuscript. We particularly want to thank Mark Thistlethwaite, associate professor of art history at Texas Christian University, who read the manuscript and gave counsel, Barbara Spielman of the University of Texas Press, who edited the catalogue, Linda K. Fetters, who produced the index, and Thomas Whitridge at Ink, Inc., who designed this handsome volume.

JAN KEENE MUHLERT, *Director*

ACKNOWLEDGMENTS

IN ADDITION to those persons mentioned in the director's foreword, the authors would like to acknowledge with gratitude the following, who kindly assisted in providing information for the catalogue:

Philip C. Beam, Bowdoin College Museum of Art
Jo-Anne Berelowitz, San Diego Museum of Art
Annette Blaugrund, The Brooklyn Museum
Jean Bellows (Mrs. Earl M.) Booth
David Brewster
Elizabeth Cheslock, The Detroit Institute of Arts
Deborah Chotner, National Gallery of Art
Amy Navratil Ciccone, The Chrysler Museum
Carol Clark, Williams College Museum of Art
Helen Cooper, Yale University Art Gallery
Joseph Czestochowski, Cedar Rapids Museum of Art
Jeanette Downing, Kimbell Museum of Art
Stephen Edidin, Montclair Art Museum
Rowland Elzea, Delaware Art Museum
Trevor J. Fairbrother, Museum of Fine Arts, Boston
Francis Farmer, Christie's London
Jim Fisher, Fort Worth Art Museum
Marilyn Florek, Archives of American Art (Detroit)
Michelle Fondas, Phillips Collection
Wolfgang M. Freitag, Fogg Art Museum
Amy Giesler, Dallas Museum of Art
Maria Graubart, Currier Gallery of Art

Kevin Grogan, Cheekwood Botanical Gardens and Fine Arts Center
Elizabeth C. Haff, Brockton Art Museum
Elizabeth H. Hawkes, Delaware Art Museum
Joseph Hawthorne
Grant Holcomb, Timken Art Gallery
William I. Homer, University of Delaware
Roger Howlett, Childs Gallery
Sona Johnston, The Baltimore Museum of Art
Sheila Klos, The Cleveland Museum of Art
Antoinette Kraushaar, Kraushaar Galleries
Cecily Langdale, Davis & Langdale Company, Inc.
Deirdre Lawrence, The Brooklyn Museum
Janet J. Le Clair
Nancy C. Little, M. Knoedler & Company
Alicia Longwell, The Parrish Art Museum
Edward Morris, Walker Art Gallery, Liverpool
Joel Myers
M. P. Naud, Hirschl & Adler Galleries
Bennard B. Perlman, Baltimore Community College
Ronald G. Pisano, Ronald G. Pisano, Inc.
Richard S. Reid, Belmont, The Gari Melchers Memorial Gallery
Donna Rhein, Dallas Museum of Art

Donna Seldin, Coe Kerr Gallery
Joan Sepessy, The Toledo Museum of Art
Cathy Shepherd, Pennsylvania Academy of the
    Fine Arts
Bernice Spandorf, Whitney Museum of Ameri-
    can Art
Rick Stewart, Dallas Museum of Art

William Tarbell
Cheryl Vogler, St. Louis Art Museum
Robert C. Vose, Jr., Vose Galleries
William B. Walker, The Metropolitan Museum
    of Art
Richard J. Wattenmaker, Flint Institute of Arts

INTRODUCTION

R ITA AND DANIEL FRAAD began looking at American art in the 1940s and purchased their first painting, Albert Pinkham Ryder's *Landscape* in 1955. That and subsequent purchases during the late 1950s—Edward Hopper's *Houses on the Beach, Gloucester*, Winslow Homer's *Prout's Neck in Winter*, Charles Hawthorne's *The Morning Coffee*, Thomas Eakins' *Study for the Portrait of Miss Emily Sartain*, and Charles Demuth's *Pepper and Tomatoes*—established the Fraads as pioneers among today's leading collectors of American art. Arthur Altschul and Herbert Goldstone in New York and the Meyer Potamkins in Philadelphia were about the only other private collectors in this field in the 1950s. Raymond and Margaret Horowitz would begin their impressive collection around 1960, and their friendship with the Fraads is reflected in a number of interesting parallels between the two collections. Jo Ann and Julian Ganz, Jr., the other leading collectors in American art, acquired their first painting in 1964.

Dealers who specialized in American art were also relatively few in the 1950s, especially when compared to the large number active today. Babcock, Abe Adler of Hirschl & Adler, Rehn, Ira Spanierman, Victor Spark, Roy Davis, Milch, Kraushaar, and Graham were among the galleries that the Fraads visited in New York on Saturdays to see and study the works on view. According to the Fraads, there was no system or philosophy behind their purchases; they followed their instincts. It is also clear that discerning eyes steered their course.

The collection grew rapidly in the early 1960s, when many of the objects in the exhibition were acquired: the two Eastman Johnson drawings; Homer's *Green Apples* and *Sand and Sky*; the Thomas Anshutz watercolor; paintings by Arthur B. Davies, Charles Sheeler, and William Merritt Chase; drawings by Joseph Stella and Jerome Myers; six works by Maurice Prendergast; John Singer Sargent's *Group with Parasols* and *A Spanish Barracks*; two works by Edward Henry Potthast; impressionist paintings by Dennis Miller Bunker, Willard Metcalf, William Glackens, and Theodore Robinson; and Ashcan works by John Sloan, Everett Shinn, George Bellows, and Robert Henri. The collection was shown publicly for the first time in 1964 at the Brooklyn Museum in an exhibition that included seventy-five objects and that subsequently traveled to the Addison Gallery of American Art, Phillips Academy, Andover, Massachusetts, but the collection has not been exhibited as a group since.

Although the core has remained intact since the Brooklyn show twenty-one years ago, a few objects have been traded, others have been given to various museums, and a number of highly significant works have been acquired. This last group includes perhaps the two greatest works that the Fraads own—Sargent's *Venetian Street* and Bellows' monumental *Shore House*. Also added since 1964 are Bellows' *The Knock Out*; Homer's watercolor *Spring*; Robinson's *The Red Gown*; Gari Melchers' *Portrait of Mrs. George Hitchcock*; and John Twachtman's *Gloucester, Fishermen's Houses*.

The Fraad collection includes works by a number of American artists at the very top of their form. Foremost in this group are the technically brilliant works by John Singer Sargent, notably his *Venetian Street* and *Group with Parasols*. The trio of early pictures—*Kids*, *The Knock Out*, and *Shore House*—by George Bellows guarantees his place in the pantheon of great American artists who depicted native scenery and people. Also shown in strength is the work of Winslow Homer, especially in his Houghton Farm watercolor, *Spring*, and that of Maurice Prendergast, who is represented by six objects (an oil, four watercolors, and a monotype) spanning approximately twenty years and chronicling his evolution in style and subject matter. John Twachtman's *Gloucester, Fishermen's Houses*, Everett Shinn's *Stage Scene*, George Luks' *The Cabby*, William Glackens' *Yellow Bath House and Sailboats, Bellport, L.I.*, and John Sloan's *Gray Day, Jersey Coast* are outstanding examples of the highest quality by these artists. The Glackens and the Sloan are especially interesting because they are types of paintings not normally associated with the artists. Stella's charcoal *Pittsburgh, Winter* is one of his most famous and often-reproduced drawings, and Gari Melchers' noble but less well known *Portrait of Mrs. George Hitchcock* is undeniably one of his finest paintings.

The Fraad collection, concentrating on the realist and impressionist artists of the late nineteenth and early twentieth centuries, is remarkable not only for its quality but also for its focus on a certain period of art history. Yet, in such works as Albert Pinkham Ryder's *Landscape*, it also reflects the rich diversity of styles during that era.

The earliest works in the show reveal the strong interest in the human figure that emerged during the last half of the nineteenth century. Realist artists, such as Eastman Johnson, Winslow Homer, and Thomas Eakins, were leaders in this movement, their subjects ranging from apple-cheeked children in the countryside to sober and penetrating character studies. Eakins' pupil Thomas Anshutz continued the tradition of realism and, through Anshutz' students (including Robert Henri, John Sloan, William Glackens, and Everett Shinn), carried the tradition into the twentieth century.

Anshutz was one of many American artists who flocked to Europe during the last half of the nineteenth century. He studied in Paris, and his work reflects the French attention to light, which fascinated a number of American painters. Other artists included in the Fraad collection—notably Frank Duveneck and Gari Melchers—were influenced by Dutch and German aesthetics. Duveneck's Munich training and love of Frans Hals is seen in his dark palette and bravura brushwork. His one-time roommate William Merritt Chase and his pupil John Twachtman eventually moved away from the Munich style to a more impressionist one, as the Fraad collection demonstrates, and Duveneck's own style would later undergo a transformation to a lighter palette and smoother facture. But the legacy of this earlier, dark, energized brushstroke continued into the twentieth century with Robert Henri and associates and with the painterly works of Charles Hawthorne, Chase's pupil and assistant.

The exhibition shows one painterly artist's work in depth, that of John Singer Sargent. The Fraads' pictures allow us to see Sargent's development, from his early powerful monochromatic work in Venice to his fluid watercolor of convalescing Spanish soldiers and one of his later colorful impressionist paintings.

American art moved from realism to impressionism at the turn of the century. The Fraad collection illustrates that change in transitional works, such as Dennis Miller Bunker's *The Station* and two works by Theodore Robinson. The academic idealization of Robinson's decorative *The Red Gown* of about 1885 stands in striking contrast to his much more naturalistic *Drawbridge—Long Branch Rail Road, Near Mianus*, painted nearly ten years later. In these two works one can see not only the evolution of an artist but also a fundamental change in national art.

Although the American Impressionists represented here—Robinson, Bunker, Twachtman, Chase,

Metcalf, and Potthast—were deeply influenced by their French counterparts, specifically in their high-keyed color, broken brushwork, and light and atmospheric effects, the American artists continued to emphasize three-dimensional form. Their styles varied, ranging from Metcalf's detailed studies of light and shadow to Twachtman's minimalist scenes, from Robinson's shimmering, atmospheric effects to Potthast's loosely rendered and generalized depictions.

Despite the prevalence of impressionism at the turn of the century, one group of New York artists in the early 1900s consciously rejected the impressionist style, preferring instead the native realist tradition of Homer, Eakins, and Johnson. The group had its germination in Philadelphia when four newspaper artists—William Glackens, John Sloan, George Luks, and Everett Shinn—came together under the charismatic leadership of Robert Henri. Moving to New York, they protested against the politics of the National Academy of Design and were joined in this effort by three artists whose styles differed from their own: Maurice Prendergast, Ernest Lawson, and Arthur B. Davies. This larger group exhibited together as The Eight in 1908.

Henri, Sloan, Luks, and Shinn—and, for a time, Glackens—concentrated on urban scenes for their subject matter and painted with a dark palette. Glackens eventually moved from the so-called Ashcan School's aesthetics to a high-keyed impressionist style, more aligned to the colorful and lyrical work of Prendergast. Arthur Davies, who had little in common with the rest of The Eight save for his protest against the Academy, was a symbolist artist. His work is more akin to the nineteenth-century visionary artist Albert Pinkham Ryder, while such artists as George Bellows and Jerome Myers—though never a part of The Eight—were actually closer in spirit and style to Henri and his followers than was Davies or Prendergast.

The Fraad exhibition also allows us to study a number of works—in a range of styles—by outstanding twentieth-century draftsmen. Most of the drawings, in addition to being exquisite in themselves, depict important and recurring subjects in the artist's career: Edward Hopper's houses; Bellows' boxers; Joseph Stella's city scene; Jerome Myers' *Self-Portrait*; Reginald Marsh's train; Charles Demuth's vegetable-and-fruit still life; and Charles Sheeler's *Shaker Barns*.

American Paintings, Watercolors, and Drawings from the Collection of Rita and Daniel Fraad moves chronologically from Eastman Johnson's drawing of about 1849 to Sheeler's *Shaker Barns* of nearly one hundred years later. The works in the exhibition tend toward the representational rather than the abstract, with the human figure and the American landscape as the primary subjects shown. But the Fraads do not intend the collection to be a survey of every American art movement. Rather, they have collected what appeals to them on an aesthetic and emotional level, and it is their individual personal taste that this exhibition embodies.

—LINDA AYRES

CATALOGUE OF THE EXHIBITION

T HE CATALOGUE consists of entries on each work in the exhibition. Artists are grouped according to major stylistic movements, with entries placed chronologically within each artist's career. Each entry is accompanied by a reproduction of the object. All known information on provenance and exhibition history has been included, as well as bibliographic references to the specific works being discussed. In the provenance listings, brackets indicate that the work was with a commercial dealer. The date on the last line in the provenance section is the date the Fraads acquired the object. All dimensions are in inches, followed by centimeters, height preceding width.

Entries for catalogue numbers 16–29 and 46–50 were written by Jane Myers. All others were written by Linda Ayres.

2.

EASTMAN JOHNSON (1824–1906)

Studies of Children, c. 1875–1880
black chalk with white heightening on tan wove paper, 7¼ × 13 in. (18.4 × 33.0 cm)
Inscribed l.r.: "E J"

PROVENANCE
[Charles Childs Gallery, Boston]
(Sale, Parke-Bernet Galleries, New York, *French and
   American Modern Paintings, Drawings, and Bronzes*,
   October 11, 1961, no. 14)
[Babcock Galleries, New York, 1961]

EXHIBITIONS
Charles Childs Gallery, Boston, n.d.

After studying in Düsseldorf, the Hague, and Paris, Eastman Johnson returned to America and eventually became one of the foremost genre painters in this country.

In 1870 Johnson began to spend the summer and fall (from late June or July to November or December) on the island of Nantucket, thirty miles off the coast of Massachusetts. He returned there each summer for nearly twenty years. The result of these visits is a group of genre scenes depicting the island residents at work and at rest. Although America was becoming industrialized during this period, Nantucket remained a rural community. Such paintings as *Cornhusking* (1876, The Metropolitan Museum of Art, New York) and *Cranberry Harvest* (1880, Timken Art Gallery, San Diego) concentrate on the agrarian aspects of island life.

For many scenes, especially in the case of Johnson's *tour de force Cranberry Harvest*, the artist often did preparatory studies of individual figures, and the sheet of studies depicting three boys probably belongs to the group of cranberry pickers Johnson sketched from the middle to late 1870s. Although the children in the Fraads' drawing are not found in the finished painting, the standing boy with uplifted arms at the right of the sheet relates to the boy with pails in the pencil-and-watercolor sketch *Berry Picking* (c. 1875–1880, Addison Gallery of American Art, Phillips Academy, Andover, Massachusetts). *Studies of Children* is a freely rendered work, with the two figures on the left sketched in summary fashion. The boy standing at the right, however, is more fully developed, with white gouache highlights to denote the areas where sunlight falls on his body.

The drawing reminds one of the country boys depicted by Winslow Homer in the 1860s and 1870s (see *Green Apples* and *Spring*, cat. nos. 3 and 4), especially in Homer's informal preliminary crayon studies, such as *Five Sketches of Young Boys* (c. 1872, Cooper-Hewitt Museum, New York).

3.

WINSLOW HOMER (1836–1910)

Green Apples (Boy Picking Apples), 1866
oil on canvas, 15 × 11 in. (38.1 × 27.9 cm)
Inscribed l.r.: "HOMER – 66 –"

PROVENANCE
George Norton Northrop, West Roxbury, Massachusetts, 1936
[Wildenstein and Co., New York, c. 1946]
Mr. and Mrs. Lawrence Fleischman, Detroit, 1954
[Hirschl & Adler Galleries, New York, 1962]

EXHIBITIONS
Prout's Neck Association, Maine, *Century Loan Exhibition as a Memorial to Winslow Homer,* 1936, no. 62, as *Boy in Orchard.*
Wildenstein, New York, *A Loan Exhibition of Winslow Homer for the Benefit of the New York Botanical Garden,* February 19–March 22, 1947, no. 10, p. 32, as *Boy Picking Apples.*
Smith College Museum of Art, Northampton, Massachusetts, *Winslow Homer: Illustrator,* February 1951; Williams College Museum of Art, Williamstown, Massachusetts, March 1951, no. 4 (illus.).

The Detroit Institute of Arts, *Collection in Progress: Selections from the Lawrence and Barbara Fleischman Collection of American Art,* 1955, no. 14, p. 17 (illus.).
Museo de Bellas Artes, Caracas, *Colección de arte norteamericano prestada por Lawrence A. Fleischman,* 1957, no. 9 (illus.). Also traveled to Greece and Israel in 1958.
Milwaukee Art Center, *American Painting, 1760–1960: A Selection of 125 Paintings from the Collection of Mr. and Mrs. Lawrence A. Fleischman, Detroit,* March 3–April 3, 1960, p. 71 (illus.).
The Brooklyn Museum, Brooklyn, New York, *American Painting: Selections from the Collection of Daniel and Rita Fraad,* June 9–September 20, 1964; Addison Gallery of American Art, Phillips Academy, Andover, Massachusetts, October 10–November 8, 1964, no. 7, pp. 14, 15 (illus.).

REFERENCES
New York Times, June 14, 1964.

Born in Boston, Winslow Homer began his career as a graphic artist. After an apprenticeship at Bufford's, a leading lithography firm in Boston, Homer became a free-lance illustrator, moving in 1859 to New York. It was in that city that he worked for *Harper's Weekly* (for whom he covered the Civil War), received his only formal artistic training, and began to paint in oil.

In addition to the Civil War scenes he created in the 1860s, Homer portrayed fashionable pastimes, such as croquet, rural life, and children at play. Children—symbols of the hope, promise, and innocence of America—were often depicted in American popular literature (Louisa May Alcott's *Little Women,* for example) and art in the nineteenth century, but they took on added significance, including nostalgia, following the traumatic years of the Civil War. Perhaps in reaction to the country's growing industrialization, these stories and paintings were often set in the countryside.

Both Homer and Eastman Johnson, who had studios in the same New York building in the 1860s, produced a number of charming studies of the joys of childhood.[1] Homer's *Green Apples* (also known as *Boy Picking Apples*) of 1866 is one such genre scene, painted in tones of brown and green, punctuated by a few red apples on the tree. The large expanse of grass creates a high horizon line and silhouettes the boy, who is rendered in a linear manner akin to Homer's illustrations. Homer was still very active as an illustrator at this time and, in fact, he used this painting two years later as the basis for a wood engraving entitled *Green Apples.* It was part of a series of illustrations featuring children at play that Homer did in

---

1. Homer may possibly have known the genre scenes of William Sidney Mount (1807–1868). John Wilmerding points out that certain compositional devices used by Homer in the 1860s and seventies recall Mount, as do the general themes of the pastimes of youth (*Winslow Homer* [New York, 1972], p. 48).

the late 1860s for a children's magazine, *Our Young Folks. Green Apples* accompanied a poem of the same title by J. T. Trowbridge, appearing in the August 1868 issue.[2]

Homer modified the composition from painting to engraving, however, pulling the young lad closer to the picture plane and adding another boy, who is seated in the background. The image appeared as an illustration again, but with the title *Porter Apples*, in a book by Horace E. Scudder, *Mr. Bodley Abroad*.[3]

A drawing entitled *Boy Picking Apples* (c. 1866, Addison Gallery of American Art, Phillips Academy, Andover, Massachusetts) is probably a transitional study between the painting and the print and features the one boy at close range in a vertical composition. A work by Homer entitled *Green Apples* was exhibited in 1875 at the American Water Color Society, but it remains unlocated.[4]

2. *Our Young Folks* 4, no. 8 (August 1868): frontispiece. The poem, "Green Apples," appeared on pp. 470–471.
3. Horace E. Scudder, *Mr. Bodley Abroad* (Boston, 1880), p. 167.
4. Helen Cooper, an authority on Winslow Homer's watercolors, does not know of any watercolor entitled *Green Apples*. She points out, however, that a review in the 1875 *Art Journal* describes "an orchard-scene, with a group of children, under a tree, eating green apples" (telephone conversation, November 27, 1984). See "American Society of Painters in Water-Colours," *Art Journal* 1 (1875): 92.

4.

WINSLOW HOMER (1836–1910)

Spring, 1878
watercolor and graphite on paper, 11 ⅛ × 8 ⅝ in. (28.3 × 22.0 cm)
Inscribed l.r.: "HOMER/1878"

PROVENANCE
Charles T. Barney, New York, c. 1878
Ashbel H. Barney, New York (Charles Barney's son)
Mrs. H. F. Dimock, Washington, D.C. (Ashbel Barney's sister)
Ashbel H. Barney (Mrs. Dimock's nephew)
[M. Knoedler & Co., New York]
Mrs. Barklie McKee Henry (Mrs. George W. Headley, Mrs. Samuel Peck), New York (Ashbel Barney's cousin), c. 1940
[Hirschl & Adler Galleries, New York, 1966]

EXHIBITIONS
Whitney Museum of American Art, New York, *Winslow Homer Centenary Exhibition*, December 15, 1936–January 15, 1937, no. 47, p. 24 (illus.).
The Walker Art Center, Minneapolis, *American Watercolor and Winslow Homer*, February 27–March 23, 1945; The Detroit Institute of Arts, April 3–May 1, 1945; The Brooklyn Museum, Brooklyn, New York, May 15–June 12, 1945, pp. 26 (illus.), 107.
Maynard Walker Gallery, New York, *Early Winslow Homer*, October 19–November 6, 1953, no. 14.
National Gallery of Art, Washington, D.C., *Winslow Homer:*

A Retrospective Exhibition, November 23, 1958–January 4, 1959; The Metropolitan Museum of Art, New York, January 29–March 8, 1959, no. 93, pp. 48 (illus.), 122.
The Metropolitan Museum of Art, New York, *200 Years of Watercolor Painting in America: An Exhibition Commemorating the Centennial of the American Watercolor Society*, December 8, 1966–January 27, 1967, no. 69, p. 16.
Whitney Museum of American Art, New York, *Winslow Homer*, April 3–June 3, 1973; Los Angeles County Museum of Art, July 3–August 15, 1973; Art Institute of Chicago, September 8–October 21, 1973, no. 88, pp. 84 (illus.), 138.

REFERENCES
Gardner, Albert Ten Eyck. *Winslow Homer, American Artist: His Life and Work* (New York, 1961), p. 120 (illus.).
Goodrich, Lloyd. *Winslow Homer* (New York, 1945), pp. 18 (illus.), 184.
———. "Winslow Homer in New York State." *Art in America* 52, no. 2 (April 1964): 82 (illus.).
Wilmerding, John. "The Last Winslow Homer Show?" *American Art Review* 1, no. 1 (September–October 1973): 62 (illus.).

In 1873 Winslow Homer saw an exhibition of British watercolors at the National Academy of Design in New York, and it was during this time that his proficiency and productivity in that medium greatly in-

creased. Beginning in 1875, Homer submitted large numbers of watercolors for exhibition, and his watercolor work became as important to him as his work in oils.

Homer lived in New York City but spent several summers in the late 1870s as the guest of his friend Lawson Valentine at Houghton Farm, in Mountainville, New York, near West Point.[1] A visit in 1878 resulted in about fifty watercolors depicting the local countryside, livestock, and, especially, the young children who lived and worked on the farms. *Spring* is one of those idyllic and fresh pastoral scenes and shows a boy and a girl—Homer often depicted pairs of figures and objects—by a rail fence near a rolling blue hill. Lawson Valentine's daughter-in-law identified the children that Homer chose to pose for him as members of the Babcock family, squatters on nearby Schunemunk Mountain.[2] Dressed in work clothes, the children symbolize American rural life.

The watercolor is beautifully rendered in quiet pastel shades of pink, blue, green, and grayish-brown. It is thinly painted, revealing Homer's underdrawing, and, in some areas, he used the white of the watercolor paper for highlights (on the girl's sunbonnet, for instance) and to indicate the patch of sky at the upper left of the composition. The transparency accounts for the work's freshness, as does Homer's ability to capture clear, outdoor light in broadly handled strokes of the brush.

The Water Color Society accepted for their 1879 spring exhibition twenty-nine of Homer's Houghton Farm watercolors, which were greeted enthusiastically by the public and the critics. The *New York Times* reviewer noted Homer's ability to "paint water-colors in a style all his own and with a vigor and individual accent that puts him away from other artists in a quite separate department." The critic continued, ". . . his pictures have a vivid, fresh originality that has on one side a childlike directness and naivete. . . . Mr. Homer has the honors of the exhibition, and must now take rank as one of the best water-colorists."[3]

1. The brothers Lawson and Henry Valentine were manufacturers of paint and varnish and owned Valentine Company, where Homer's brother Charles was employed as chief chemist. The Valentines were Winslow Homer's early patrons as well, buying many of the Houghton Farm scenes. See Lloyd Goodrich, *Winslow Homer in New York State* (Mountainville, N.Y., 1963), pp. 7–8.
2. Gordon Hendricks, *The Life and Work of Winslow Homer* (New York, 1979), p. 138. These same children are also seen in the 1878 watercolors *Feeding Time* (Sterling and Francine Clark Art Institute, Williamstown, Massachusetts), *Two Children in a Field* (Museum of Fine Arts, Boston), and *On the Stile* (Mrs. Harold T. Pulsifer, on loan to Colby College, Waterville, Maine). The setting of *On the Stile* is identical to that of *Spring*.
3. *New York Times*, February 1, 1879, quoted in Hendricks, *The Life and Work of Winslow Homer*, p. 139. Because of generalized titles, it is difficult to tell if *Spring* was included in this particular exhibition. There was a watercolor entitled *Girl and Boy*, but this could refer to any number of watercolors.

5.
WINSLOW HOMER (1836–1910)

Sand and Sky (Carrying Catch along a Beach), 1887
watercolor and graphite on paper, 13⅜ × 19⅛ in. (34.0 × 48.5 cm)
Inscribed l.l.: "Winslow Homer 1887"

PROVENANCE
Philip Henry Brown, Portland, Maine
Philip Greely Brown (Philip Henry Brown's son), 1893
Estate of Philip Greely Brown
(Sale, Parke-Bernet, American Art Association, Anderson
    Galleries, New York, *American and French Paintings*,
    November 1, 1935, no. 15, illus.)
Emil Schwartzhaupt, New York, 1935
Estate of Leo Gerngross
[Hirschl & Adler Galleries, New York, 1962]

EXHIBITIONS
American Water Color Society, New York, *Twenty-First
    Annual Exhibition*, 1888, no. 500, as *Sand and Sky*.
The Brooklyn Museum, Brooklyn, New York, *American*

*Painting: Selections from the Collection of Daniel and Rita
Fraad*, June 9–September 20, 1964; Addison Gallery of
American Art, Phillips Academy, Andover, Massachu-
setts, October 10–November 8, 1964, no. 8, p. 16
(illus.).
Pembroke College Club of New York, Amel Gallery, *A
Contemporary Art Exhibit from the private collections of
Brown and Pembroke Alumni and Friends of the University*,
April 18, 1965, n.p.

REFERENCES
"Fine Arts: Pictures at the Water-Color Exhibition." *The
    Nation*, February 23, 1888, p. 163.
"The Gallery: Exhibitions of the Water-Color Society and
    the Etching Club." *Art Amateur*, March 1888, p. 82.

In 1881 Homer went to England, where he spent a year and a half in the fishing village of Cullercoats on the Northumberland coast. The large number of watercolors he executed there (he worked primarily in that medium in England) are more somber in mood and palette than his earlier efforts. Many depict the sturdy women of Cullercoats, carrying baskets, mending fishing nets, or watching the sea for the return of their husbands.

After Homer's return to America, he settled in 1883 in a village reminiscent of Cullercoats—Prout's Neck, Maine, about twelve miles south of Portland.[1] There he transformed a stable into a studio and home, which overlooked the steep cliffs and ocean. This would be his main residence for the last three decades of his life. It was Prout's Neck that provided the inspiration for many of Homer's masterful seascapes. Although Homer's marine scenes are perhaps the best known images of his later work, the artist by no means abandoned the human figure as subject matter, as evidenced by the people who inhabit his colorful Adirondack and Caribbean watercolors as well as some of his Prout's Neck work.

Some of the Maine watercolors, including *Sand and Sky* of 1887, continue the theme of fisherwomen that Homer began in England in the early 1880s. *Sand and Sky* depicts two young girls carrying a large basket along the dunes, probably in the area of Black Rock, Eastern Point, on the northern side of Prout's Neck.[2] Although the women look strong, they are not the monumental figures that dominate Homer's British compositions (for example, *Inside the Bar*, The Metropolitan Museum of Art, New York), but appear more elegant and feminine. The gray and misty coastal atmosphere of the Northumbrian scenes pervades this work, although the watercolor paper that Homer allows to show through lends a luminosity to the sandy dunes and beach.

Sand and Sky was favorably received at its initial exhibition at the American Water Color Society in 1888. A reviewer for *The Nation* considered Homer the most original painter in the show—"not so much in mere choice of subject matter as in his manner of presenting it artistically"—and described *Sand and Sky* as "an effective study. . . remarkable for its virility of style."[3] The critic for the *Art Amateur* found the watercolor to be one of Homer's "best and most characteristic works."[4]

1. Charles L. Homer, Winslow's nephew, told Philip Beam that the artist wanted to live and work in a setting similar to Cullercoats. The Homer family had summered in Prout's Neck since 1875. See Philip C. Beam, *Winslow Homer at Prout's Neck* (Boston, 1966), p. 27.
2. Philip Beam believes that the dunes resemble most closely those found near Black Rock, Eastern Point, and seen in the painting entitled *The Wreck* (1896, Museum of Art, Carnegie Institute, Pittsburgh). He reports that Homer used several local girls as models—Addie Kaler Vaill, Cora Sanborn, Louise Libby, and Ida Meserve. Addie Vaill and Ida Meserve told Beam that Homer used them interchangeably and generalized them, so that it is difficult to identify the women in *Sand and Sky* (letter, November 8, 1984, Philip Beam to Linda Ayres; I am extremely grateful to Professor Beam for his comments on Winslow Homer's work, especially that done at Prout's Neck).
3. "Fine Arts: Pictures at the Water-Color Exhibition," *The Nation*, February 23, 1888, p. 163.
4. "The Gallery: Exhibitions of the Water-Color Society and the Etching Club," *Art Amateur*, March 1888, p. 82. Homer's watercolors of 1887–1889 sold better than his oils. See Lloyd Goodrich, *Winslow Homer* (New York, 1945), p. 101.

6.

WINSLOW HOMER (1836–1910)

Prout's Neck in Winter, c. 1892
oil on canvas mounted on board, 12½ × 22⅝ in. (31.7 × 57.5 cm)

PROVENANCE
Martha (Mrs. Charles S.) Homer (sister-in-law of the artist)
Maria W. Blanchard, October 1918
Ralph Whittier, Bangor, Maine, 1936 (Miss Blanchard and
   Whittier's mother were Homer's cousins)
Whittier Estate
[Rebecca C. J. Jackson, New Boston, New Hampshire,
   1950]
[Maynard Walker, New York]
[Babcock Galleries, New York, 1956]

EXHIBITIONS
Fieldstone School Arts Center, Fieldstone, New York,
   Collector's Choice, March 31–April 3, 1957, no. 7.
The Brooklyn Museum, Brooklyn, New York, *American
   Painting: Selections from the Collection of Daniel and Rita
   Fraad*, June 9–September 20, 1964; Addison Gallery
   of American Art, Phillips Academy, Andover,
   Massachusetts, October 10—November 8, 1964, no. 9, p.
   17 (illus.).

Homer lived at Prout's Neck nearly year round, and his works created there depict the area's rocks, dunes, beaches, surf, and pastures in different seasons, weather, light, and moods.[1] Although Homer spent the coldest months painting in the warmer climates of Florida, Bermuda, or the Bahamas, he was usually in Maine until at least December, and his letters sometimes indicate the harsh weather and a tinge of lone-

1. Philip C. Beam, *Winslow Homer at Prout's Neck* (Boston, 1966), pp. 34, 60.

liness—"These are tough days. Very cold; deep snow."[2] *Prout's Neck in Winter* and other local winter scenes[3] are even more revealing of the desolation and bitter bleakness of a Maine winter.

Prout's Neck in Winter, a panoramic scene of a winter sunrise, is austere, yet serenely beautiful, presented with an economy of means and an innate sense of design. It is a pure landscape, devoid of all human presence. Wide horizontal bands divide the composition, yet the overall subdued tonalities (Whistlerian grays and browns) cause the snow-covered land, sea, and sky to merge into one. The painting is a majestic landscape, composed of near-abstract elements and imbued with a love of the rugged Maine seacoast. In its broad handling of form and color, it is akin to Ryder's *Landscape* (cat. no. 7) of the 1890s.

The looseness, small size, and directness of *Prout's Neck in Winter* indicate that it may have been painted outdoors. It has been suggested that this painting may have served as a preliminary study for *The Fox Hunt* (Pennsylvania Academy of the Fine Arts), begun in Maine in March 1893.

2. Lloyd Goodrich, *Winslow Homer* (New York, 1945), p. 108.
3. Others include *The West Wind*, 1891 (Addison Gallery of American Art, Phillips Academy, Andover, Massachusetts), *Winter Coast*, 1890 (Philadelphia Museum of Art), and *Coast in Winter*, 1892 (Worcester Art Museum).

7.
ALBERT PINKHAM RYDER (1847–1917)

Landscape, 1890s
oil on canvas, 9 × 13 in. (22.9 × 33.0 cm)

PROVENANCE
Colonel Charles Erskin Scott Wood, Los Gatos, California
Mrs. Kirkham Smith, San Rafael, California (daughter of C. E. S. Wood)
[Maynard Walker, New York]
[Babcock Galleries, New York, 1955]

EXHIBITIONS
[Possibly] Babcock Galleries, New York, *Selected Intimate Paintings by American Artists*, December 1946, no. 1.
San Diego Museum of Fine Arts, San Diego, California, *Representative Nineteenth-Century American Paintings and Decorative Arts*, January 6–February 8, 1952, no catalogue.

The Brooklyn Museum, Brooklyn, New York, *American Painting: Selections from the Collection of Daniel and Rita Fraad*, June 9–September 20, 1964; Addison Gallery of American Art, Phillips Academy, Andover, Massachusetts, October 10–November 8, 1964, no. 12, p. 20 (illus.).

REFERENCES
Price, Frederic Newlin. *Ryder* (New York, 1932), no. 76.
Sherman, Frederic Fairchild. *Albert P. Ryder* (New York, 1920), no. 122, p. 73.

Born in the whaling town of New Bedford, Massachusetts, the visionary painter Albert Pinkham Ryder moved to New York around 1870, where he lived for the rest of his life. He received little formal artistic training, although he studied under William Marshall and at the National Academy of Design, where he began to exhibit in 1873. In 1877 he helped to establish the Society of American Artists and exhibited with that group through the 1880s.

Ryder traveled to London briefly in 1877 and went to London, Paris, Spain, Italy, Tangier, and the Alps in 1882. He went abroad again in later years, although it is said these trips were mainly for the sea voyage.

Known in his own time and today as an eccentric recluse, Ryder, who was plagued by chronic eyesight problems, created a body of work that is highly imaginative and evocative. His small-scale paintings

were not in the mainstream of American art, but, as Charles Eldredge has pointed out, they can be seen as related to the earlier subjective romanticism of Washington Allston, John Quidor, and William Page and to the later nineteenth-century American artists George Fuller, Elihu Vedder, and John LaFarge.[1] Although most American landscapes were concretely realistic and objective and often depicted nature in great detail (as in the work of Thomas Cole, Asher B. Durand, and Frederic E. Church), Ryder's paintings take us into the realm of mysticism and what Lloyd Goodrich has termed "landscapes of the inner mind."[2]

Ryder's 1890s *Landscape* is based on the naturalistic world, but the artist has simplified the components into broad masses of color (mainly dark browns), generalized forms, and rhythmic movement. These elements in Ryder's work call to mind the suggestive monochromatic nocturnes of James McNeill Whistler. Ryder, in fact, favored nocturnal subjects, either moonlight or twilight, that evocative and poetic time between day and night. *Landscape* is an expressive study of twilight, with its transluscent sky aglow, and invites prolonged reflection and meditation from the viewer.

1. Charles C. Eldredge, *American Imagination and Symbolist Painting* (New York, 1979), p. 35. Eldredge notes (p. 37) that the tendency toward idealism and introspective imagination at the end of the nineteenth century was international in scope.
2. Lloyd Goodrich, *Albert Pinkham Ryder* (Washington, D.C., 1961), p. 10. Ryder's work is almost impossible to date; he never dated his paintings.

8.

THOMAS EAKINS (1844–1916)

Study for the Portrait of Miss Emily Sartain, c. 1890–1895
oil on canvas, 23½ × 17½ in. (59.7 × 44.5 cm)

PROVENANCE
Emily Sartain, Philadelphia
Emily Sartain Estate, Philadelphia
Harriet Sartain, Philadelphia
Harriet Sartain Estate, Philadelphia
(Sale, Samuel T. Freeman and Co., Philadelphia, June 13, 1957, no. 503)
[Babcock Galleries, New York, 1957]

EXHIBITIONS
The American Academy of Arts and Letters, New York, *Thomas Eakins, 1844–1916,* January 16–February 16, 1958, no. 52, n.p.
The Brooklyn Museum, Brooklyn, New York, *American*

Painting: Selections from the Collection of Daniel and Rita Fraad, June 9–September 20, 1964; Addison Gallery of American Art, Phillips Academy, Andover, Massachusetts, October 10–November 8, 1964, no. 13, p. 21 (illus.).

REFERENCES
Goodrich, Lloyd. *Thomas Eakins* (New York, 1933), no. 478 or 479, p. 206.
————. *Thomas Eakins* (Cambridge, Mass., 1982), I: 44.
Hendricks, Gordon. *The Life and Work of Thomas Eakins* (New York, 1974), p. 37 (illus., fig. 35).
Schendler, Sylvan. *Eakins* (New York, 1967), pp. 145, 216 (illus., fig. 69).

America's greatest nineteenth-century portraitist, Thomas Eakins, lived most of his life in Philadelphia, where his friends included the Sartain family, prominent in artistic circles. William Sartain, son of the mezzotintist, editor, and publisher John Sartain, was Eakins' boyhood friend from Central High School and a fellow student at the Pennsylvania Academy of the Fine Arts. Will's sister Emily (1841–1927), three years older than Eakins, became a portrait painter and mezzotint engraver, and Eakins was in love with her during the 1860s.

Eakins parted from Emily Sartain in 1866, when he left for Paris to study at the Ecole des Beaux-Arts. Although they corresponded and exchanged photographs, the letters became strained and less frequent with time, and the relationship came to an end.[1] Emily Sartain swore she would never marry, and she never did.

Eakins and Miss Sartain remained friends, however. In fact, it was Eakins who was instrumental in Emily Sartain's appointment, in 1886, as principal of the Philadelphia School of Design for Women, America's first school of industrial art established for women. A handsome person of great intelligence and determination, Sartain led the school until her death.

Although Lloyd Goodrich reports that Eakins painted two unfinished portraits of Emily Sartain in the 1890s, this painting is the only one known today. It was probably meant to be a study for a large, full-length work that was never painted, perhaps because, as it has been suggested, Miss Sartain proved to be too "bossy" a sitter.[2] It is understandable that Eakins would want to paint Sartain's portrait, not only because of their long-standing friendship but also due to Eakins' admiration for professional women. His portraits of female singers, actresses, musicians, and educators attest to that interest.[3]

After Eakins' forced resignation as professor of the Pennsylvania Academy in 1886, the artist concentrated more on portraiture, dealing less frequently with such earlier themes as genre, sporting, and

1. For Thomas Eakins' relationship with Emily Sartain and copies of some of their correspondence, see Lloyd Goodrich, *Thomas Eakins* (Cambridge, Mass., 1982), I: 14–15, 40–44.
2. Ibid., I: 44. John Wilmerding, in "Thomas Eakins' Late Portraits," *Arts* 53, no. 9 (May 1979): 112, states that unfinished paintings by Eakins were rare before 1895.
3. See, for example, Eakins' portraits of Weda Cook, Suzanne Santje, Edith Mahan, and Lucy L. W. Wilson.

historical scenes.[4] It was during the 1890s that Eakins asked several female friends, including Emily Sartain, to pose for him. The women he painted are thinking, active women, so different from the ethereal, idealized madonnas then being portrayed by such artists as Thomas Wilmer Dewing or Abbott H. Thayer or the women in the flashy society portraits exemplified by the work of John Singer Sargent. Eakins did not paint the conventional ideals of beauty, perhaps one of the main reasons for his lack of portrait commissions. His likenesses were not meant to flatter.

In *Study for the Portrait of Miss Emily Sartain*, the figure, dressed in a cream-colored evening dress, emerges from a dark brown, ambiguous space. The background is composed of boldly painted areas and ghostlike outlines of a large piece of furniture (a secretary or breakfront), a rug, and a chairback, on which Miss Sartain rests her outstretched right arm. Her arms, in fact, are only roughed in, and her bodice is freely and sketchily painted. The emphasis is on the serious and dignified face of the sitter, for it is only the head—the source of thought in the body—that has been developed fully in this painting.

Miss Sartain confronts the viewer directly with a penetrating gaze. Her bearing is commanding and erect, her expression serious, almost stern. Yet coupled with this no-nonsense stare are eyes capable of great feeling, compassion, sadness, and loneliness. She looks ill at ease in the frilly ball gown, probably worn at Eakins' request. Even in an unfinished work such as this, Eakins has probingly sought out and captured the essential character and individuality of the sitter.

4. The controversy surrounding Eakins' insistence on teaching from male nudes in female classes led, in part, to his departure from the Academy.

9.

THOMAS ANSHUTZ (1851–1912)

Two Boys by a Boat—Near Cape May, 1894
gouache, wash, and graphite on wove paper, 13¼ × 19⅞ in. (33.6 × 50.5 cm)
Inscribed on verso: "Near Cape May 1894 by / Thomas P. Anshutz ANA / Edward R. Anshutz
Artist's Son"

PROVENANCE
Anshutz Estate
[James Graham & Sons, New York, 1963]

EXHIBITIONS
Graham Gallery, New York, *Thomas Anshutz,*
    February 19–March 16, 1963, no. 70, illus., n.p.
The Brooklyn Museum, Brooklyn, New York, *American*
    Painting: Selections from the Collection of Daniel and Rita
    Fraad, June 9–September 20, 1964; Addison Gallery of
    American Art, Phillips Academy, Andover, Massachu-
setts, October 10–November 8, 1964, no. 17, p. 25
(illus.).
The Metropolitan Museum of Art, New York, *200 Years of*
    Watercolor Painting in America: An Exhibition Commemo-
    rating the Centennial of the American Watercolor Society,
    December 8, 1966–January 29, 1967, no. 100, p. 20.

REFERENCES
The Brooklyn Museum. *Summer Bulletin,* 1964.
Hoopes, Donelson F. *American Watercolor Painting* (New
    York, 1977), pp. 62, 81 (illus.).

Fig. 1. Thomas Anshutz, *Three Boys by a Boat—Maurice River*, photograph, c. 1894. Thomas Anshutz Papers, Collection Archives of American Art, Smithsonian Institution.

Thomas Anshutz, who served as the artistic link between Thomas Eakins and The Eight, studied at the National Academy of Design in New York beginning in 1872 and at the Pennsylvania Academy in 1876, where he later became an assistant to Thomas Eakins. After Eakins' forced resignation from the Academy, Anshutz took over his teacher's classes and taught there for over thirty years, succeeding William Merritt Chase as director in 1909. His students, known as "Tommyites," included future members of The Eight (Robert Henri, John Sloan, William Glackens, and Everett Shinn) as well as such artists as John Marin, Morton Livingston Schamberg, Charles Sheeler, and Charles Demuth, whose art would take a different, more abstract, direction.

Anshutz' *Ironworkers: Noontime* (c. 1880–1881, Fine Arts Museums of San Francisco), a realistically painted genre scene of newly industrial America, reflects Eakins' naturalism and looks ahead to the work that would be done by the early twentieth-century realists known as the Ashcan School. Anshutz was not to continue painting this type of industrial subject matter, however, and after a trip to Europe in 1892–1893, his style changed.

In Paris, he studied at the Académie Julian and probably saw contemporary exhibitions of the work of Renoir, Pissarro, Seurat, Degas, and others. Anshutz keenly felt the impact of the French Impressionists and their ability to capture the effects of light and certain times of day. It was also at this time that he became increasingly interested in the medium of watercolor.

A group of watercolors executed the year following his return from Paris reflect his new concern for outdoor light. The subject of the series is young boys and sailboats at Holly Beach, New Jersey, on the Maurice River near the mouth of the Delaware River.[1] *Two Boys by a Boat—Near Cape May* is a large and impressive example of Anshutz' new style, a type of innovative and evocative work that would influence such students as Sheeler and Demuth, two premier watercolorists of the early twentieth century.[2]

An overall pinkish tonality pervades the work, which is divided into minimalistic, transparent bands

1. While in Paris and concerned about his financial condition, Anshutz wrote to his brother Edward: "I feel very anxious to make a living outside of teaching. And see no better scheme than to go to Holly Beach and turn out a lot of water color pictures of the Seashore etc." (cited in Ruth Bowman, "Thomas Pollock Anshutz, 1851–1912" [unpublished master's thesis, New York University, 1971], n. 43). Bowman reports that during the 1890s Anshutz went on long sketching expeditions by sailboat in the creeks around Delaware Bay, western Pennsylvania, and Cape May.
2. See Sandra Leff's essay in Graham Gallery, *Thomas Anshutz: Paintings, Watercolors and Pastels* (New York, 1979), p. 3.

of blue, yellow, green, pink, and tan washes arranged parallel to the picture plane. Everything reflects the strong summer light: the sky, water, sand, and grassy shore; the fleshy pink skin of the boys; the asymmetrically placed gaff-rigged catboat with its sparkling white boom and mast hoops; the pile of clothes between the two boys; and the shimmering image of a group of children in the background with another boat.

The watercolor reveals not only Anshutz' deft handling of impressionistic light effects and his ability to capture a specific moment in time, but it also shows Thomas Eakins' legacy in its ordered composition and its solid study of the structure of the human form. The horizontal bands of color, mentioned above, are balanced by the verticals provided by the mast of the boat and the standing boy. The composition is strictly and geometrically ordered, with the figures placed in a strong diagonal line leading from the beach grass to the mast.

Anshutz participated in the locomotion photography experiments carried out at the University of Pennsylvania in the early 1880s by Eadweard Muybridge and Thomas Eakins, and it is known that Anshutz, like his teacher, often used photographs as a working aid. A photograph of three boys by a cat-boat (fig. 1) confirms that Anshutz used it as a study for the image in the Fraad collection, as well as for two related watercolors, *Two Boys by a Boat* (Collection of Raymond and Margaret Horowitz, New York) and *Two Boys by a Boat (Cape May)* (Museum of Art, Carnegie Institute, Pittsburgh). The composition of the watercolors, however, has been simplified by the deletion of one of the boys who appeared in the photograph.[3]

In the Holly Beach watercolors, no action occurs, only stillness and contemplation and an almost nostalgic feeling for childhood days at the seashore.

3. Ruth Bowman, "Nature, the Photograph, and Thomas Anshutz," *Art Journal* 33, no. 1 (Fall 1973): 32–40.

II.

GARI MELCHERS (1860–1932)

Portrait of Mrs. George Hitchcock, c. 1890
oil on canvas, 35½ × 21¾ in. (90.2 × 55.3 cm)
Inscribed u.r.: "Gari Melchers"

PROVENANCE
Henriette Hitchcock (later Henriette Lewis-Hind), London
Mr. Doward, England (possibly C. G. Doward)
[Hirschl & Adler Galleries, New York, 1957]
Dr. and Mrs. Irving F. Burton, Detroit, 1957
(Sale, Sotheby Parke Bernet, New York, *Highly Important
    19th and 20th Century American Paintings, Watercolors
    and Drawings*, October 18, 1972, no. 27)

EXHIBITIONS
World's Columbian Exposition, Official Catalogue, Fine Arts,
    Chicago, 1893, no. 717, p. 28, as *Portrait of Mrs. H.*
Berlin, *Grosse Berliner Kunst-Ausstellung*, 1895, no. 1135,
    p. 61, as *Die Stickerin.*
Berlin, *Grosse Berliner Kunst-Ausstellung*, May 5–September 16, 1900, no. 853, as *Die Stickerin.*
The Detroit Institute of Arts, *Gari Melchers: A Centenary
    Exhibition*, February 16–March 13, 1960, no. 6, cover
    (illus.).
The Detroit Institute of Arts, *American Paintings and
    Drawings from Michigan Collections*, April 10–May 6,
    1962, no. 108, pp. 8, 22 (illus.).
Flint Institute of Arts, Flint, Michigan, *American Painting,
    1860–1960*, March 1961.
Art Gallery of Toronto, *American Painting, 1865–1905*,

January 6–February 5, 1961; Winnipeg Art Gallery
Association, February 17–March 12, 1961; Vancouver
Art Gallery, March 29–April 23, 1961; Whitney
Museum of American Art, New York, May 17–June 18,
1961, no. 49, p. 54, as *Portrait of a Woman.*
Graham Gallery, New York, *Gari Melchers, 1860–1932,
    American Painter*, September 26–October 28, 1978,
    no. 17.
The Metropolitan Museum of Art, New York, *American
    Drawings, Watercolors and Prints*, May 19–August 11,
    1980.

REFERENCES
Artist's Notebook, as *Mrs. Hitchcock Stickerin.*
Dinnerstein, Lois. "The Industrious Housewife: Some
    Images of Labor in American Art." *Arts Magazine* 55
    (April 1981): 109–119, illus. p. 114.
Dreiss, Joseph G. *Gari Melchers: His Works in the Belmont
    Collection* (Charlottesville, Va., 1984), p. 187.
Oresman, Janice. "Gari Melchers' Portrait of Mrs. George
    Hitchcock." *Archives of American Art Journal* 20, no. 3
    (1980): 19 (illus.)–24.
Wutsch, Ludwig. "The Great Art Exhibition." *Vossische
    Zeitung* (Berlin), no date [sometime in 1900].

An international portraitist and figure painter known for his depictions of Dutch peasants, Gari Melchers was born in Detroit, the son of a German wood carver and sculptor. Melchers studied for four years in Düsseldorf and, in 1881, went to Paris for further training at the Ecole des Beaux-Arts and the Académie Julian. He moved in 1884 to Egmond-aan-zee, a rural fishing village on the North Sea in Holland, where he shared a studio with George Hitchcock, a friend from his days in Paris.

It was in this studio that Melchers produced some of his finest paintings, works that he exhibited widely and that brought him fame and numerous awards. While Hitchcock concentrated primarily on landscapes, Melchers' interest was the human figure.

Hitchcock's wife, Henriette (known as "Miggles"), often modeled for Melchers and is the subject of an arresting work in the Fraad collection, *Portrait of Mrs. George Hitchcock.*[1] Typical of this period in Melchers' career and of his Düsseldorf training, the scene is a darkened interior, painted with a subdued palette, with an interest in firm modeling, textures, and capturing facial expressions.

Mrs. Hitchcock's noble, solid figure emerges from a rich teal blue background, clothed in a dark green dress. Light focuses our attention on her face, richly modeled and profiled against the wall and a salmon-colored painting above. Attention is also drawn to the sitter's right hand, her wrist edged in fine

1. Janice Oresman, "Gari Melchers' Portrait of Mrs. George Hitchcock," *Archives of American Art Journal* 20, no. 3 (1980): 19–24.

black lace, her hand ornamented by a gold-and-turquoise ring and etched with blue veins. She is depicted as a cultivated woman of leisure, with silver thimble, needle, and embroidery frame (providing a bright abstract floral motif at lower right), linked together by an orange thread that crosses her front, paralleling the line of her smock.

The theme of the virtuous housewife with needle and thread goes back to colonial portraiture in American art, but the subject took on other connotations in the late nineteenth century. Needlework, an activity appropriate to expectant mothers, became a discreet allusion to pregnancy (for example, William Merritt Chase's *For the Little One*, 1892, The Metropolitan Museum of Art, New York). On closer inspection, it becomes apparent that Mrs. Hitchcock's dress is actually an elegant maternity outfit.[2]

The portrait dates prior to the 1890s when Melchers' style changed to one of overall decorative patterning and brighter tonality (seen in his later portrait of Mrs. Hitchcock, *The Delft Horse*, 1900, Belmont, Fredericksburg, Virginia). In the earlier painting, the centralized figure is realistically and academically rendered, and the character of the sitter is sensitively portrayed as she gazes into a space beyond the picture frame. The stillness of this carefully composed domestic scene calls to mind the work of the Dutch artist Vermeer, whom Melchers admired, but its space is cropped in the manner of the French artists Manet and Degas, whose work Melchers must have seen during his studies in Paris.

Portrait of Mrs. George Hitchcock was a pivotal work in the artist's career. After its exhibition at the World's Columbian Exposition in 1893, Melchers received a number of important commissions.

Henriette and George Hitchcock were divorced in 1905, and she left Holland, eventually settling in England. In 1907, she married the British critic and writer Charles Lewis Hind. Henriette Lewis-Hind remained Melchers' close friend, became his London dealer, and wrote a monograph on the artist in 1928. She died in England in 1937, when this painting was still in her possession.

2. For a discussion of the theme of women sewing in American art, see Lois Dinnerstein, "The Industrious Housewife: Some Images of Labor in American Art," *Arts Magazine* 55 (April 1981): 109–119.

12.

JOHN SINGER SARGENT (1856–1925)

Venetian Street, c. 1880–1882
oil on canvas, 29 × 23¾ in. (73.7 × 60.3 cm)
Inscribed l.l.: "John S. Sargent"

PROVENANCE
Benoît-Constant Coquelin, Paris, by 1888
(Sale, Galerie Georges Petit, Paris, *Tableaux Modernes, Aquarelles, Pastels, Dessins Composant La Collection Coquelin*, May 27, 1893, no. 54, as *A Seville*)
Dr. Leo C. Collins, Paris (bought at auction in Europe)
[Paris dealer]
[Victor Spark, New York, 1955]
[Grand Central Art Galleries, New York, 1956]
Arthur Vining Davis (1867–1962), Pittsburgh and Miami
Private collection

[David David Gallery, Philadelphia]
[Hirschl & Adler Galleries, New York, 1964]

EXHIBITIONS
Grand Central Art Galleries, New York, 1956.
Whitney Museum of American Art, New York, *Art of the United States: 1670–1966*, September 28–November 27, 1966, no. 248, p. 153.
The Metropolitan Museum of Art, New York, *New York Collects: Paintings, Watercolors and Sculpture from Private Collections*, July 3–September 2, 1968, no. 200, p. 23.

Coe Kerr Gallery, New York, *Americans in Venice, 1879–1913*, October 19–November 16, 1983, no. 31, pp. 17–18, 49 (illus.).

REFERENCES
Les Lettres et Les Arts, July 1888, p. 92 (illus.).
Mount, Charles Merrill. "Carolus-Duran and the Development of Sargent." *Art Quarterly* 26, no. 4 (1963): 399.

The cosmopolitan artist John Singer Sargent was born in Italy to American parents. His artistic training occurred in Rome, Florence, and Paris and in travel to other cities to study the Old Masters. Sargent joined his family in Venice in September 1880, fresh from his studies in Paris with the portraitist Emile Auguste Carolus-Duran. He stayed at least through January 1881, working in the Palazzo Rezzonico, where James McNeill Whistler and Giovanni Boldini also had studios. In the summer of 1882 he made a second trip to Venice, lasting three or four months. During this visit, Sargent stayed in the Palazzo Barbaro with his Boston relatives, the Daniel Curtis family.

In these two Venetian sojourns, Sargent created a remarkable series of genre paintings that form a distinct body of work from his early career. *Venetian Street* ranks as one of the finest works in that group.

Sargent's figure paintings reflect a different view of Venice than those created by numerous other American artists (Maurice Prendergast, Thomas Moran, Sanford Robinson Gifford, to name but a few) who worked in the city in the late nineteenth century.[1] Sargent was not drawn to the festive crowds, architectural monuments, or grand canals at this point in his career but instead concentrated on the people of the lower classes, talking in the side streets or working indoors.

These intimate, monochromatic, and fairly austere scenes focus on a small number of figures placed in deeply receding spaces. The painting in the Fraad collection, also known as *Flirtation Lugubre*, captures a romantic, mysterious meeting of a man and woman in an alley, or *calle*, its narrowness emphasized by the vertical canvas.

The same two figures—an unidentified man and Gigia Viani, Sargent's favorite Venetian model—appear again in other Venetian scenes: *A Street in Venice* (Sterling and Francine Clark Art Institute, Williamstown, Massachusetts); *Street in Venice* (National Gallery of Art, Washington, D.C.); and *Sulphur Match* (Jo Ann and Julian Ganz, Jr., Los Angeles). The National Gallery's painting is known to depict Calle larga dei Proverbi, and, although the location of the Fraads' painting has not yet been identified, it may well depict the same general area in the northern part of Venice, near the Church of Santi Apostoli.[2]

Venetian Street is subtly and thinly painted in blacks and grays, although Gigia's white skirt picks up a range of pink hues and her blouse is magenta. The walls, where architectural elements are kept to a minimum so as not to detract from the figures, have touches of pink, blue, and brown. A pearly light infuses the whole canvas. Sargent's love of light-dark contrasts is seen in his placement of the figures, clad in coal black cloak and shawl, against light walls, in the dark shutters and hanging clothes (or "friperies") that punctuate the building's surfaces, and in the white cat and bright street light in the background.

A comparison of *Venetian Street* with an oil study for the painting (20½ × 16⅜ inches, private collection, fig. 2) reveals a number of changes that Sargent made when painting the larger work. The cat and the couple at the left rear (echoing the main protagonists at the right foreground) have been added,

1. Two recent exhibitions have chronicled the phenomenon of American artists in Venice. See Donna Seldin, *Americans in Venice, 1879–1913* (New York, 1983), and Margaretta Lovell, *Venice: The American View, 1860–1920* (San Francisco, 1984).
2. Venice is made up of an endless maze of such *calles*. Although David McKibbin (letter to Daniel Fraad, July 28, 1971) thought that the Fraad painting depicted the poor Castello section, the rear building's open upper window and the barred storeroom window below identify it as a palazzo, the home of a nobleman (I thank C. Douglas Lewis at the National Gallery of Art for this observation).

Fig. 2. John Singer Sargent, *Study for Venetian Street*, c. 1880–1882, oil on canvas, 20½ × 16⅜ inches, private collection. Photograph courtesy of Sotheby's, New York.

Fig. 3. Dressing room of Coquelin at Comédie-Française taken in 1888. Sargent's *Venetian Street* hangs to the right of the fireplace. Photograph courtesy of the Cleveland Museum of Art.

while a woman on the balcony has been deleted, as have several windows and other architectural details to the wall at the right of the canvas.

Sargent's Venetian genre scenes are indebted to the somber and subdued works of Whistler, who also portrayed the Venetian working class in alleyways. One can also see the influence of the free brushwork of Frans Hals and Velásquez' mysterious space and prevalent use of the color black (Sargent went to Spain and Holland in 1879–1880 to study Hals and Velásquez).[3]

An 1888 photograph (fig. 3) of the Comédie-Française dressing room of the renowned actor Benoît-Constant Coquelin shows the Fraad painting (in reverse) hanging on the wall.[4]

3. Sargent's debt to Velásquez was noted by critics as early as 1882. See, for instance, "The Salon: From an Englishman's Point of View," *Art Journal* 44 (July 1882): 219.
4. The photograph appeared in *Les Lettres et Les Arts*, July 1888, p. 92. Coquelin (1841–1909) was the actor who created the role of Cyrano de Bergerac.

13.
JOHN SINGER SARGENT (1856–1925)
Studies for Venetian Street Scenes, c. 1880–1882
pen and ink on paper, 13¾ × 9¼ in. (34.9 × 23.5 cm)

PROVENANCE
Curtis Family, Venice
Mrs. Ralph W. Curtis, Paris
Sylvia Curtis Steinert (later Mrs. Schuyler Owen), Paris
    (daughter of Mrs. Ralph W. Curtis)
Theodore A. C. Steinert, Paris (son of Sylvia Curtis
    Steinert), 1965
(Sale, Parke-Bernet Galleries, New York, *American Paint-
    ings, Drawings & Sculpture of the 18th, 19th, and Early
    20th Century*, October 27–28, 1971, no. 87, p. 39.

This pen-and-ink series of studies depicts the man who appears, clad in a dark, fur-collared cape, in sev-eral Venetian genre scenes by Sargent. The pose at upper left most closely resembles the stance of the male figure in *Venetian Street* (cat. no. 12).

Although it has been proposed that the model for this figure was the American artist J. Frank Cur-rier, that identification is doubtful. Nelson White, who has written a book about Currier and who has corresponded extensively with Currier's descendants, does not believe that Currier posed for Sargent's paintings. According to Mr. White, Sargent and Currier met only once or twice, and not in Venice.[1]

The happy indolence of the Venetian dandy, like the one shown in these sketches, was observed by a number of American visitors to the city, including the artist Francis Hopkinson Smith, who described the handsome, mustachioed men in their "Leporello" hats.[2]

The sheet of drawings descended in the family of Ralph Curtis, an artist and distant cousin of Sargent's, with whom Sargent stayed when visiting Venice in 1882 and later years. Their home, the fifteenth-century Palazzo Barbaro, became a salon for the Anglo-American group in Venice. Henry James and Isabella Stewart Gardner were both visitors to Palazzo Barbaro.

1. Nelson White, in a telephone conversation to Linda Ayres, June 14, 1982.
2. F. Hopkinson Smith, *Gondola Days* (Boston and New York, 1897), p. 31.

14.

JOHN SINGER SARGENT (1856–1925)

A Spanish Barracks, c. 1903
watercolor and graphite on paper, 11⅞ × 17⅞ in. (30.2 × 45.4 cm)
Inscribed u.r.: "to my friend Dr. Hugh Playfair / John S. Sargent 1906"

PROVENANCE
Dr. Hugh Playfair, London
Mrs. Hugh Playfair, London, 1928
Major General I. S. O. Playfair (Dr. Playfair's nephew),
    1928
(Sale, Christie's, London, *Modern Prints and Drawings and
    a few Paintings*, July 9, 1963, no. 33, as *Three Men Seated
    on the Pavement of a Sunlit Portico*)
[Hahn, 1963]
[John Nicholson Gallery, New York, 1963]

EXHIBITIONS
[Possibly] Royal Society of Painters in Water-Colours,
    Centenary Exhibition, summer 1904, no. 86, p. 22.
[Possibly] Carfax Gallery, London, April 1905, no. 4.
Walker Art Gallery, Liverpool, Royal Society of Painters in
    Water Colours, *Liverpool Autumn Exhibition*, 1922, no.
    730, p. 48, as *The Hospital*.

The Brooklyn Museum, Brooklyn, New York, *American
    Painting: Selections from the Collection of Daniel and Rita
    Fraad*, June 9–September 20, 1964; Addison Gallery of
    American Art, Phillips Academy, Andover, Massachu-
    setts, October 10–November 8, 1964, no. 29, p. 37
    (illus.).
Pembroke College Club of New York, Amel Gallery, *A
    Contemporary Art Exhibit from the private collections of
    Brown and Pembroke Alumni and Friends of the University*,
    April 18, 1965, n.p.
The Metropolitan Museum of Art, New York, *200 Years of
    Watercolor Painting in America: An Exhibition Commem-
    orating the Centennial of the American Watercolor Society*,
    December 8, 1966–January 29, 1967, no. 106, p. 20.

REFERENCES
Ormond, Richard. *John Singer Sargent: Paintings,
    Drawings, Watercolors* (New York, 1970), p. 250.

Although this watercolor is dated with the year 1906, it may well have been executed several years earlier
and inscribed at the time it was presented as a gift to Dr. Hugh Playfair, a London obstetrician.[1] Sargent
was in northern Spain in 1902 and 1903 in search of ideas and images for his mural project at the Boston
Public Library. While at Santiago de Compostela in 1903, he created a small series of watercolors depicting Spanish soldiers relaxing at the Hospital Real (for example, the Brooklyn Museum's *Spanish Soldiers*,
c. 1902–1903, and *Group of Convalescent Soldiers*, c. 1903, in the collection of the Richmond family,
England). David McKibbin identified the setting for *A Spanish Barracks* as one of the southern courts of
the hospital, a Renaissance structure that had been modernized in the 1880s.[2]

    In *A Spanish Barracks*, a group of four men, three seated in a semicircle (perhaps playing a game) on

1. Sargent depicted various members of the Playfair family, and his portrait of Mrs. William Playfair is in the Fraad collection
(although not in the current exhibition).
2. Sargent's letters place him at Santiago de Compostela in August 1903. See James Lomax and Richard Ormond, *John Singer
Sargent and the Edwardian Age* (London, 1979), p. 95. David McKibbin's identification of the setting can be found in a letter
from Mr. McKibbin to Daniel Fraad, dated September 1966.

the pavement and one standing at far right, are seen in the architectural setting of the hospital courtyard. Columns, doors, and niches divide the space vertically, while the long lines of shadows provide horizontal divisions. The light brown of the architecture is punctuated by Sargent's deft use of color, evidenced by red pants on two of the figures and bluish shadows.

Sargent often painted watercolors in a single session, normally done on dry paper. He first roughly sketched the subject in pencil—traces of underdrawing can be seen in the figure to the far right and the column behind—and then applied washes of transparent color with large brushes or sponges.[3] Sargent freely drew the objects in this watercolor with fluid movements, and one senses that the central figural group (seen again in a diagonal, close-up formation in Brooklyn's *Spanish Soldiers*) was very quickly rendered. The artist did not indicate the features of the soldiers' faces, for it was not his intention to record their identity. Rather, the watercolor is a study of light and shadow, of bright summer light and reflections.

Sargent painted watercolors mainly for his own pleasure and exhibited them publicly less often than his oils. The watercolors, as in the case of *A Spanish Barracks*, were frequently dedicated to his friends.

3. Richard Ormond, *John Singer Sargent: Paintings, Drawings, Watercolors* (New York, 1970), p. 70.

15.
JOHN SINGER SARGENT (1856–1925)

Group with Parasols (A Siesta), c. 1903–1911
oil on canvas, 21¾ × 27⅞ in. (55.2 × 70.8 cm)
Signed l.r.: "[illeg.] John S. Sargent"

PROVENANCE
(Sale, Christie, Manson & Woods, London, *Pictures and
Water Colour Drawings by J. S. Sargent, R. A. and Works
by Other Artists*, July 27, 1925, no. 194, as *A Siesta*)
Leonard Fred Harrison, London, 1926
Wilfred G. de Glehn, London
A. Richards, London
(Sale, Sotheby & Co., London, *Modern British Drawings,
Paintings, and Sculpture*, December 13, 1961, no. 128)
[John Nicholson Gallery, New York, 1961]
[Hirschl & Adler Galleries, New York, 1962]

EXHIBITIONS
[Possibly] Carfax Gallery, London, 1903, as *A Siesta*.
Royal Academy of Arts, London, *Exhibition of Works by the
Late John S. Sargent, R. A.*, Winter 1926, no. 3.
[Possibly] Royal Academy of Arts, London, *British
Paintings since Whistler*, 1940, no. 460.
The Brooklyn Museum, Brooklyn, New York, *American
Painting: Selections from the Collection of Daniel and Rita*

Fraad, June 9–September 20, 1964; Addison Gallery of
American Art, Phillips Academy, Andover, Massachu-
setts, October 10–November 8, 1964, no. 30, p. 38
(illus.).
Whitney Museum of American Art, New York, *Art of the
United States: 1670–1966*, September 28–November 27,
1966, no. 246, pp. 69 (illus.), 153.
The Metropolitan Museum of Art, New York, *100th
Anniversary of Impressionism*, December 10, 1974–
February 16, 1975, not in catalogue.

REFERENCES
Charteris, Evan. *John Sargent* (New York, 1927), p. 295.
Lomax, James, and Richard Ormond. *John Singer Sargent
and the Edwardian Age* (London, 1979), p. 97.
McKibbin, David. *Sargent's Boston* (Boston, 1956), p. 100.
Mount, Charles Merrill. *John Singer Sargent: A Biography*
(New York, 1955), K1216, p. 451.
Ormond, Richard. *John Singer Sargent: Paintings,
Drawings, Watercolors* (New York, 1970), p. 75.

By 1900, John Singer Sargent was the foremost portraitist in England and America, but he was growing weary of portrait painting. His lucrative career, however, allowed him to go on three-to-four-month sketching holidays, often with a large group of family members and friends, trips he took annually until the outbreak of World War I. Sargent and his entourage headed for the Alps during the hot summer months and then down to the plains of Italy or Spain in the autumn.[1]

On these holidays, Sargent sketched almost ceaselessly, and a large number of light-filled landscape and figure studies in watercolor and oil resulted. Many works depict Sargent's traveling companions— his sisters, Emily and Violet, and Violet's family, and an assortment of London friends, such as the Harrisons, Stokeses, de Glehns, and Barnards. Sargent would carefully arrange the figures in casual poses and sometimes in exotic costumes, as he did in *Dolce Far Niente* (c. 1908–1909, The Brooklyn Museum, Brooklyn, New York).

One theme he painted was a group of figures asleep *al fresco*, among the rocks and trees. Although a number of watercolors of this subject are known, the magnificent painting in the Fraad collection, *Group with Parasols*, is believed to be the only one rendered in oils.[2]

Although the date of the painting is uncertain due to the frequency with which Sargent and his friends returned to certain retreats, the painting's creation was remembered by one of the four partici-pants, Lilian Mellor (later Mrs. Hare), who believed it to have been in 1905: "Our party at G[iomein] was Mr. and Mrs. Peter Harrison. . . Leonard Harrison, Dos Palmer, Sargent and myself." Sargent did

1. James Lomax and Richard Ormond, *John Singer Sargent and the Edwardian Age* (London, 1979), p. 93.
2. *The Siesta* and *A Siesta*, numbers 84 and 85 respectively, in the catalogue for *John Singer Sargent and the Edwardian Age* are watercolors. *The Siesta* depicts the Harrison brothers, also seen in the Fraad painting.

an "oil sketch of me in the centre, with Leonard Harrison's head on my lap and Peter and Dos in it too."[3] The painting, however, could date as early as 1903, when a work by Sargent entitled *A Siesta* was exhibited in London, or conceivably as late as 1911.[4]

   Group with Parasols is a *tour de force* in its decorative design and Sargent's handling of paint and vibrant color to depict the bright summer sunlight and shadow. The figures, which occupy most of the canvas, are placed close to the picture plane. Mrs. Palmer (far left) and Miss Mellor, their parasols shad-

3. Quoted in *John Singer Sargent and the Edwardian Age*, p. 97. The brothers Lawrence Alexander ("Peter") Harrison (1866–1937) and Leonard Fred ("Ginx") Harrison (1870-c. 1939) were Sargent's London friends and sketching companions. Mrs. Dorothy Palmer was Peter Harrison's mistress and owned several Sargent portraits of Harrison. Giomein is a small village above Breuil on the Italian side of the Matterhorn. It has also been suggested that the setting of the painting is Purtud, a village at the head of the Val d'Aosta on the Italian side of Mt. Blanc, where Sargent often sketched. See Richard Ormond, *John Singer Sargent: Paintings, Drawings, Watercolors* (New York, 1970), p. 75.

4. Donna Seldin of the John Singer Sargent *Catalogue Raisonné* project at Coe Kerr Gallery currently dates the work about 1911 on stylistic grounds. However, she reports that the date has not yet been pinned down and may well be changed to an earlier one (telephone conversation, Donna Seldin and Linda Ayres, January 11, 1985).

ing their faces and their long white dresses reflecting a spectrum of colors, and Leonard and Peter Harrison (far right) almost blend into the landscape itself. The figures and trees all catch the flickering patterns of bright sunlight and deep shadow. Textures of flesh, foliage, clothing, and rock are varied and form an animated surface. It is as if Sargent's brush never stopped moving in building up the forms on the canvas. The impasto is exceptionally rich and thick, notably on the hat in the foreground, the bodice of Mrs. Palmer's dress, and Peter Harrison's shirt, right leg, and shoe.

The languid pose of the figures exudes a sense of total abandonment and the luxurious feeling of the freedom of a holiday siesta.

16.
DENNIS MILLER BUNKER (1861–1890)

The Station, c. 1886–1889
oil on canvas, 14 × 18 1/16 in. (35.6 × 45.9 cm)
Inscribed l.r.: "TO TARBELL / D. M. BUNKER"

PROVENANCE
Mary Tarbell Schaffer, New Castle, New Hampshire
[Giovanni Castano, Boston]
[Ira Spanierman, New York, 1964]

EXHIBITIONS
The New Britain Museum of American Art, Connecticut, *Dennis Miller Bunker (1861–1890) Rediscovered*, April 1–May 7, 1978; Davis & Long Company, New York, June 7–30, 1978, no. 14, n.p.

Inscribed by Dennis Miller Bunker to fellow artist Edmund Tarbell, *The Station* represents the view out of Bunker's Boston studio at 145 Dartmouth Street, the present site of Back Bay Station. The painting was probably executed in the winter of either 1886–1887 or 1888–1889, when both Bunker and Tarbell were young art instructors in Boston.

Bunker was raised on Long Island. Classes at the National Academy of Design and the Art Students League in New York were followed by a trip to France in 1882 and courses at the Académie Julian and the Ecole des Beaux-Arts. In 1885, Bunker took a position at Boston's Cowles Art School, where he also had living quarters, and Tarbell, Bunker's junior by one year, worked in a nearby studio.[1]

In *The Station*, a bleak winter's day is rendered in a painterly manner recalling the example of William Merritt Chase, one of Bunker's instructors at the Art Students League. The composition and subject matter, as well as the expressive brushwork, point to the work of Edouard Manet, Claude Monet, and their contemporaries who had legitimized the railroad station as subject matter. The Frenchmen favored a similar boulevardlike space flowing into the foreground, the elevated vantage point resulting in the high horizon line and the tilted appearance of the picture plane. Like the French Impressionists, Bunker conveyed his interest in atmospheric variations attending the change of season. Winter provided the even, gray light conditions preferred by Bunker who, in 1886, lamented the "distressingly bright" days and yearned for a "solemn sky and a grey world."[2]

1. See Patricia Jobe Pierce, *Edmund C. Tarbell and the Boston School of Painting, 1889–1980* (Hingham, Mass., 1980), p. 232, n. 6. Pierce indicates that Tarbell may have taught briefly at Cowles. It is also possible that Bunker made Tarbell's acquaintance at the Académie Julian, where they were both enrolled in 1883.
2. Letter to Ann Page, September 1, 1886, Dennis M. Bunker correspondence, Archives of American Art, Smithsonian Institution, microfilm roll 1201.

The gray tonality matched the artist's mood, for Bunker's letters of this period reveal a self-disparaging, poverty-stricken, and ailing artist, who made his home in Boston only reluctantly. Bunker spent his idle moments in the studio contemplating the Boston and Albany railroad, a regular fixture of his quotidian existence: "If the Boston and Albany Road which passes directly under my window doesn't drive me quite mad I hope to get to work very soon."[3] Bunker longed to travel to what he considered to be the more stimulating environs of New York or Europe and, in this respect, the train served as a metaphor for escape. "A train has just slipped past my window bound for New York," he wrote to a friend. "Alas, it carries my heart with it."[4]

In 1888, Bunker's wishes were realized when he traveled to England with his friend John Singer Sargent, whose expressive brushwork and brilliant color schemes are credited with the pronounced shift in Bunker's painting style toward a more impressionistic manner from that time forward.

3. Letter to Joe Evans, October 2, 1886, Dennis M. Bunker correspondence, Archives of American Art, Smithsonian Institution, microfilm roll 1201.
4. Letter to Joe Evans, February 1887, Dennis M. Bunker correspondence, Archives of American Art, Smithsonian Institution, microfilm roll 1201.

17.

THEODORE ROBINSON (1852–1896)

The Red Gown (His Favorite Model), c. 1885
oil on canvas, 75½ × 38½ in. (191.8 × 97.8 cm)

PROVENANCE
Florence A. Robinson (sister-in-law of the artist), 1912
[Macbeth Gallery, New York, 1919]
John F. Braun, Philadelphia
(Sale, Kende Galleries, New York, *Fine Paintings from the
    Collection of the late John F. Braun*, January 16, 1942,
    no. 78, as *His Favorite Model*)
[John Douthitt Gallery, New York]
[Giovanni Castano, Boston]
[Francis Moro, New York]
[Hirschl & Adler Galleries, New York, 1965]

EXHIBITIONS
The Memorial Art Gallery, University of Rochester,
    Rochester, New York, *The Inaugural Exhibition*,
    October 8–29, 1913, no. 106, p. 30.
Macbeth Gallery, New York, *A Collection of Paintings by
    Deceased American Artists*, March 11–30, 1914, no. 21
    (illus.).

The Buffalo Fine Arts Academy, Albright Art Gallery,
    *Catalogue of the Ninth Annual Exhibition of Selected Paint-
    ings by American Artists*, May 16–August 31, 1914, no.
    98, p. 18.
Wickersham Gallery, New York, *Exhibition of Oils,
    Drawings, and Watercolors*, October 9–30, 1965,
    no. 24, n.p., as *His Favorite Model*.
The Metropolitan Museum of Art, New York, *New York
    Collects: Paintings, Watercolors and Sculpture from Private
    Collections*, July 3–September 2, 1968, no. 196, p. 23.

REFERENCES
Baur, John I. H. *Theodore Robinson, 1852–1896* (Brooklyn,
    1946), pp. 26, 74.
Macbeth Gallery, New York. *Paintings by American Artists
    and Colonial Portraits* (c. 1914), no. 193, pp. 80
    (illus.)-81.

Born in Vermont and raised in Wisconsin, Theodore Robinson received his early training at the Art Institute of Chicago and the National Academy of Design in New York. He later broke with the Academy and
was a founding member of the Art Students League. In 1876, like many of his fellow aspiring artists, he
traveled to France to study with leading figures of the Parisian art academies. Three years later, Robinson
returned to America and settled in New York, where he supported himself by teaching and by assisting
prominent designers John LaFarge and Prentice Treadwell in various decorative commissions. In 1884,
Robinson made a second trip to France, where he was to spend much of his career, and became an important disseminator of French Impressionism among his American colleagues. *The Red Gown* dates to this
second sojourn in France when Robinson worked side by side with Barbizon and impressionist artists in
the artistic enclaves of Fountainbleau, Giverny, and Grez. Shortly after returning to France he executed a
series of paintings devoted to female figures in outdoor settings.

Schooled in the academic curriculum with its emphasis on three-dimensional modeling of the human
figure, Robinson uses subtle, tight brushstrokes to define the curvilinear outlines of the model's face,
hands, and red gown, whose simplified form recalls some indeterminable historical past. Popularized in
England during the late nineteenth century, the single, standing female figure became integrated into the
aesthetic of contemporary interior design schemes that Robinson had practiced in New York. The vocabulary of the American decorator is also indicated by the monumental scale, the compressed and shallow
space, and the languid timelessness of the figure, who expresses neither emotion nor narrative.[1]

Although the subject of female figures placed in a landscape was continued by Robinson after the
mid-1880s, subsequent works in this series, such as *La Vachère* (1888, Baltimore Museum of Art), while

1. Linda Ferber has also pointed out the relationship between *The Red Gown* and Whistler's *Symphony in Flesh Color and Pink:
Portrait of Mrs. Francis Leland* (1871–1874, Frick Collection, New York). Robinson knew Whistler in Venice in 1879 (letter to
Daniel Fraad, December 12, 1973).

retaining the large scale of *The Red Gown*, mark Robinson's contact with the French Impressionist Claude Monet, his neighbor in Giverny, where the younger artist had moved in 1888. These slightly later efforts evince a concern for definition of actual time and place based on firsthand observation of nature. In addition, the model evolves into a more convincingly French peasant type, occupied with a domestic chore, and the subject becomes integrated within a landscape setting.

The model of *The Red Gown* resembles Marie, a French girl with whom Robinson was romantically linked.[2] Marie's enduring popularity with the artist is perhaps reflected in the alternate title the painting has assumed over the years, *His Favorite Model*.

2. There are at least two studies for the head of the model in *The Red Gown*, one in oil (Moussa Domit, *American Impressionist Painting* [Washington, D.C., 1973], illus. p. 112) and one in watercolor (Sona Johnston, *Theodore Robinson, 1852–1896* [Baltimore, 1973], illus. p. 8).

18.

THEODORE ROBINSON (1 8 5 2 – 1 8 9 6)

Drawbridge—Long Branch Rail Road, Near Mianus, 1894
oil on canvas, 12 × 17⅞ in. (30.5 × 45.4 cm)

PROVENANCE
Estate of the artist
(Robinson estate sale, American Art Association, New York, March 24, 1898, no. 75)
J. B. Mabon, New York
[Davis Galleries, New York, 1962]

EXHIBITIONS
Macbeth Gallery, New York, *Theodore Robinson*, February 2–16, 1895, no. 16.
Cotton States and International Exposition, Atlanta, 1895, no. 529.
St. Louis Museum of Fine Arts, *A Collection of 27 Pictures and Studies by Theodore Robinson*, 1896, no. 14.

Fort Wayne Art School, Fort Wayne, Indiana, *Central Art Association Exhibit*, 1896, no. 29.
Cincinnati Museum Association, *A Collection of Work by the Late Theodore Robinson*, 1897, no. 12.
The Brooklyn Museum, Brooklyn, New York, *American Painting: Selections from the Collection of Daniel and Rita Fraad*, June 9–September 20, 1964; Addison Gallery of American Art, Phillips Academy, Andover, Massachusetts, October 10–November 8, 1964, no. 19, p. 27.

REFERENCES
Baur, John I. H. *Theodore Robinson, 1852–1896* (Brooklyn, 1946), no. 55, p. 61.

In 1892 Theodore Robinson returned from France to the United States, where he remained until his premature death four years later. In his native country, he sought to uncover a distinctive American character in his own work, which, he believed, was tied to a deeper emotional commitment to his painting: "I have not *felt* my subjects. This year I got back among the hills I knew when a boy—I was born in Vermont—and I am just now beginning to paint subjects that touch me."[1]

To this end, between 1892 and 1894, Robinson frequented the area around Greenwich, Connecticut, where he visited fellow Impressionists J. Alden Weir and John Twachtman, the founder of an art colony in nearby Cos Cob, a picturesque village off Long Island Sound. Robinson spent several months in Cos Cob during the summer of 1894 and painted a number of small, sensitively handled works devoted to the boats dotting the harbor. Suffering from frail health much of his life, he seemed to be revitalized by the relaxed routine of the art community. In his diary, he wrote, "Am getting well and strong and work with

1. Hamlin Garland, "Theodore Robinson," *Brush and Pencil* 4, no. 6 (September 1899): 285.

interest—especially from R. R. Bridge."[2] This structure, pictured in *Drawbridge*, spans the Mianus River near Cos Cob and served as a subject for Robinson; as his diary indicates, he painted from the bridge as well.[3]

As suggested by the drawing of this scene from his sketchbook dated September 1894, the artist's initial conception was a structural and geometric one.[4] To add dimension to these simple forms Robinson modulates his limited color range over a dark ground, his thick brushstrokes emphasizing the forms of the boats, which caught his eye: ". . . walked around by the R. R. bridge to Mianus and back. . . some fine things—little white boats near the sound—anchored, also at Mianus, with the R. R. Bridge in the distance."[5] The distinctive shimmering atmospheric quality he achieved was noted by critics reviewing the artist's 1895 exhibition, in which over twenty paintings and drawings, including *Drawbridge*, appeared. Organized by Macbeth Gallery, it subsequently traveled to Atlanta, St. Louis, Fort Wayne, and Cincinnati.

2. Diary entry, June 19, 1894, quoted in Sona Johnston, *Theodore Robinson, 1852–1896* (Baltimore, 1973), p. vii.
3. *Low Tide; Riverside Yacht Club* (1894, Collection of Mr. and Mrs. Raymond J. Horowitz) may have been taken from the vantage point of the bridge. See *American Impressionist and Realist Paintings and Drawings from the Collection of Mr. & Mrs. Raymond J. Horowitz* (The Metropolitan Museum of Art, 1973). As pointed out by Sona Johnston, the bridge also appears in the background of Robinson's *E. M. J. Betty* (1894, private collection) (letter to Jane Myers, November 27, 1984).
4. Private collection. Illustrated, Johnston, *Theodore Robinson*, p. 73.
5. Diary entry, June 7, 1894, quoted in John I. H. Baur, *Theodore Robinson, 1852–1896* (Brooklyn, 1946), p. 41.

19.

WILLIAM MERRITT CHASE (1849–1916)

Landscape, Shinnecock Hills, c. 1898–1900
oil on canvas, 16 × 20 in. (40.6 × 50.8 cm)
Inscribed l.r.: "Wm M Chase"

PROVENANCE
Graham Williford, New York
Mrs. Ellen Maguire
[Kraushaar Galleries, New York]
[Hirschl & Adler Galleries, New York, 1962]
Gift of William and Lewis Fraad, 1962

EXHIBITIONS
The Brooklyn Museum, Brooklyn, New York, *American*

Painting: Selections from the Collection of Daniel and Rita Fraad, June 9–September 20, 1964; Addison Gallery of American Art, Phillips Academy, Andover, Massachusetts, October 10–November 8, 1964, no. 16, p. 24 (illus.).

The Vatican Museums, Braccio di Carlo Magno, Vatican City State, *A Mirror of Creation: 150 Years of American Nature Painting,* September 24–November 23, 1980, no. 33, n.p.

A prominent painter who played an active role in the New York art community in the late nineteenth and early twentieth centuries, William Merritt Chase enjoyed an equally important career as an art teacher and served on the faculty of several leading art academies. In 1891 when Chase took the innovative step of establishing the Shinnecock School of Art, near Southampton, Long Island, he set a precedent for future American summer schools where students could gather for instruction from an established master in an outdoor setting. At Shinnecock, Chase tutored over one hundred students each summer in the coloristic effects of sunlight on natural forms. *Landscape, Shinnecock Hills* is one of many *plein air* paintings of dunes, grasses, and sky that Chase executed during these sessions, which continued through 1902.[1]

Born in Indiana, Chase began his artistic career in St. Louis, where he benefited from local patronage enabling him to study in Munich during the mid-1870s. Through exposure to works of the Masters, he perfected his considerable technical agility as evidenced in his portraits and still lifes. Such studio works, which he continued through his later career, retain much of the spontaneity typical of the Munich School but contrast with the dazzling landscapes executed at Shinnecock. In the 1880s, Chase began to lighten his palette and to execute *plein air* renderings of parks in the New York area. Even freer in spirit than these outdoor studies of the 1880s are the Shinnecock landscapes, where a fully realized subject is secondary to a study of variations in atmospheric conditions rendered in loosely handled brushstrokes. Like his other depictions of this area, *Landscape, Shinnecock Hills,* reveals the artist's concern for achieving convincing perspective through variation in paint application and sweeping diagonals, played against an undulating horizon line, broken only by occasional shrubbery.[2]

1. Because Chase's Shinnecock landscapes are numerous and many bear similar titles, it is difficult both to date them and to distinguish among their individual exhibition histories.
2. See, for example, the closely related landscape *Shinnecock Hill* (c. 1892, oil on canvas, 20 × 46½ inches) in the collection of the University of Georgia Museum of Art.

20

JOHN HENRY TWACHTMAN (1853–1902)

Gloucester, Fishermen's Houses, c. 1900
oil on canvas, 25 × 25½ in. (63.5 × 64.8 cm)

PROVENANCE
Mr. and Mrs. Godfrey Twachtman, Independence, Missouri
[Ira Spanierman, New York, 1967]

EXHIBITIONS
Cincinnati Art Museum, *A Retrospective Exhibition: John*

Henry Twachtman, October 7–November 20, 1966, no. 86, p. 19, lent by Mr. and Mrs. Godfrey Twachtman, Independence, Missouri.
Ira Spanierman Gallery, New York, *John Henry Twachtman, 1853–1902: An Exhibition of Paintings & Pastels*, February 3–24, 1968, no. 24, n.p.

A founding member of the Ten American Painters, John Henry Twachtman conducted art classes for three summers beginning in 1900 at the popular artists' haunt, Gloucester, Massachusetts.[1] Known for his landscape subjects, which ranged from poetic and subtle tonal renderings of the French countryside to bold, vigorous depictions of Yellowstone and Niagara Falls, Twachtman devoted his final artistic phase, represented by the canvases executed in Gloucester, to the habitat of the coastal fishermen.

To render the broad planes of weather-beaten architecture and the patterns formed by riggings of the ships docked along the wharves, Twachtman employed enthusiastic and exaggerated brushwork. The expressive quality of his paint is associated with that of his teacher, Frank Duveneck, with whom Twachtman worked in Cincinnati, native city of both artists. Twachtman also traveled with Duveneck in Munich and Venice in the 1870s and worked with him in Gloucester. However, Duveneck's Gloucester works are characterized by more traditional compositions and greater solidity of form than are those of his younger colleague.

In his Gloucester canvases, Twachtman achieves an increasingly personal style. As the artist focuses on houses that fill the square format of the painting, "the spirit of the scene not the letter" reaches its ultimate form.[2] Similar to *Harbor View Hotel* (1902, Nelson-Atkins Museum of Art, Kansas City, Missouri), believed to be Twachtman's last work, *Gloucester, Fishermen's Houses* evinces a nervous energy created by a barrage of pronounced diagonals veering out of the picture plane. The texture of the rapidly applied paint modulates from thick impasto of the laundry swaying in the breeze to thinly painted passages throughout the work where the ground has been allowed to show through, thereby enhancing the hurried, rhythmic effect. The color scheme is restricted to a few bold hues—red, violet, and green—which, although the pigment is used sparingly, imparts a sense of solidity and volume to the architecture.[3]

1. The Ten American Painters, many of whom worked within an impressionist mode, sought to liberate American art from what they perceived to be the strictures of figural, studio work. They withdrew from the Society of American Artists and, in 1898, instituted a series of exhibitions featuring work by their members.
2. Katharine Metcalf Roof, "The Work of John Henry Twachtman," *Brush and Pencil* 12, no. 4 (July 1903): 245.
3. The red hue that dominates the painting suggests identification of this work with checklist no. 307 in Phillip Hale, "The Life and Creative Development of John H. Twachtman" (unpublished Ph.D. diss., Ohio State University, 1957), p. 461:

RED HOUSE. Whereabouts unknown.
25 × 25. Painted summer 1900.
Descrip.: Houses in middle foreground, steps on right side. No trees. Immediate foreground perhaps water. This is one of the Gloucester paintings seen only as thumbnail sketch by artist after original work. Title by Twachtman.

21.

WILLARD LEROY METCALF (1858–1925)

The Little White House, 1919
oil on canvas, 24⅛ × 24⅛ in. (61.3 × 61.3 cm)
Inscribed l.r.: "w. l. metcalf. 1919"

PROVENANCE
The artist
[Milch Galleries, New York]
H. Egginton, New York
[Victor Spark, New York, 1963]

EXHIBITIONS
Milch Gallery, New York, *Exhibition of Paintings by Willard L. Metcalf*, March 15–April 3, 1920, no. 14, cover (illus.).
The Corcoran Gallery of Art, Washington, D.C., *Paintings by Willard L. Metcalf*, January 3–February 1, 1925, no. 21.

The Brooklyn Museum, Brooklyn, New York, *American Painting: Selections from the Collection of Daniel and Rita Fraad*, June 9–September 20, 1964; Addison Gallery of American Art, Phillips Academy, Andover, Massachusetts, October 10–November 8, 1964, no. 21, p. 29 (illus.).

REFERENCES
Teevan, Bernard. "A Painter's Renaissance." *International Studio* 82 (October 1925): 10, illus. as *White House*.

The year in which Willard Leroy Metcalf painted *The Little White House* also marked the final joint exhibition of the Ten American Painters (a group Metcalf had helped found with John Henry Twachtman twenty years earlier) at the Corcoran Gallery of Art in Washington, D.C. Although more vital art movements had eclipsed the novelty of the Impressionists' approach, Metcalf's artistic powers remained undiminished and he continued to produce works representing his cherished New England countryside with the approbation of both art critics and collectors.

A native of Lowell, Massachusetts, Metcalf began his training in the Boston art schools. In 1883, he went abroad and received additional academic schooling at the Académie Julian in Paris, and, in the village of Giverny, he associated with Claude Monet and the American artists Theodore Robinson and John Henry Twachtman. Returning to the United States in 1889, Metcalf settled in New York, where he worked as an illustrator and conducted art classes at Cooper Union.

Responding to the Ten's emphasis on American subjects and a direct confrontation of nature, Metcalf gradually laid aside his Barbizon-influenced works and embraced the lighter palette and broken brushwork of the Impressionists. A trip to Maine in 1903 proved to be the turning point in his artistic life whereupon he renounced his New York-based career and moved to New England.

Singled out by contemporary critics for his allegiance to naturalistic form, Metcalf endeavored to capture the salient features of the scenes he painted. His landscapes were praised for their allusions to the indigenous character of the region: "Willard Metcalf's work portrays the most characteristic aspect of the Eastern states in the terms of a thoroughly American temperament."[1] An embodiment of a New England spring, *The Little White House* was praised on the occasion of its exhibition at the Milch Galleries in 1920, when a reviewer applauded the painting's "demure cottage, its commendable bushes, its tumble down fence and the fragrant waverings of its blossoming fruit trees . . . worth a chapter in itself."[2]

Like other American Impressionists, Metcalf sought to maintain integrity of form while simultaneously depicting the transitory moment. Recalling the work of Childe Hassam—who, with Metcalf, was a

1. Catherine Beach Ely, "Willard L. Metcalf," *Art in America* 13, no. 6 (October 1925): 332.
2. John H. Raftery, "Paintings by Metcalf," *New York Telegraph*, March 31, 1920, Willard L. Metcalf Papers, Archives of American Art, Smithsonian Institution, microfilm roll N70–13, frame 544.

leading figure in the Old Lyme, Connecticut, art colony—the feathery brushstrokes impart a dappled, flickering effect to the light as it filters through the leaves. The purple and green shadows, learned from Monet's example, serve as anchors in this well-ordered composition, which includes Metcalf's favored device, a diagonal (here a meandering fence), which proportionally demarcates the space in a logical recession.

22

EDWARD HENRY POTTHAST (1857–1927)

Beach Scene, c. 1915–1920
oil on panel, 11¾ × 15¾ in. (29.9 × 40.0 cm)
Inscribed l.r.: "E. Potthast"

PROVENANCE
Dr. Martin G. Dumler, Cincinnati
[James Graham & Sons, New York, 1962]

EXHIBITIONS
The Brooklyn Museum, Brooklyn, New York, *American*

Painting: Selections from the Collection of Daniel and Rita Fraad, June 9–September 20, 1964; Addison Gallery of American Art, Phillips Academy, Andover, Massachusetts, October 10–November 8, 1964, no. 22, p. 30 (illus.).

A prodigious recorder of recreational life along the beaches of the northeastern United States, Edward Henry Potthast rendered sun-filled canvases in numerous variations during the first quarter of the twentieth century.[1] By that time the seashore had been explored as subject matter by Winslow Homer and William Merritt Chase, as well as the contemporary Spanish artist Joaquín Sorolla y Bastida. The atmospheric beach scenes of the nineteenth-century French realist Eugène-Louis Boudin also have strong stylistic and compositional parallels with Potthast's paintings.

Although Potthast was nearly an exact contemporary of several of the impressionist artists who founded the Ten American Painters, he was a relative latecomer to their method and did not exhibit with them during the 1880s and 1890s when their movement was gaining critical attention. A native of Cincinnati, Potthast studied at both the McMicken School of Design and the Cincinnati Museum Association Art School, where he was influenced by fellow Cincinnati artist Frank Duveneck to develop subjects from daily life rendered in expressive brushstrokes. Potthast supplemented this early schooling with trips abroad, notably a three-year sojourn in Munich in the 1880s. Shortly after he relocated in New York City in 1896, Potthast's earlier training gave way to the atmospheric spontaneity and brilliant colors of the Impressionists, as seen in his typically small-scale *Beach Scene*.

The chronology of Potthast's beach scenes is difficult to ascertain, for they are rarely dated, but a survey of Potthast's entries at art annuals over a twenty-year period, as well as his few dated works, indicates a progressive loosening of style. In contrast to works like *Bathers* (c. 1913, The Brooklyn Museum, Brooklyn, New York), where the artist focuses on a small group of figures, the artist in *Beach Scene* retreats to a more distant vantage point, and the entire landscape—sea, sand, and sky—becomes the subject of the picture. Potthast has reduced the scene to a series of parallel bands, where figures in gaily colored bathing attire are situated along the low horizon line, their individuality blurred by the impasto brushstrokes.

1. Although the exact locations of these subjects are only occasionally identified, some were executed on the spot along the beaches near New York City. Other paintings depict the New England coast, where Potthast traveled during the summer months.

23.

EDWARD HENRY POTTHAST (1857–1927)

A Summer's Night, c. 1920–1925
oil on board, 15¾ × 19¾ in. (40.0 × 50. 2 cm)

PROVENANCE
Mr. Murray, New York (purchased from an unknown New
   York dealer)
[Wickersham Gallery, New York, 1962]

EXHIBITIONS
Wickersham Gallery, New York, *The Transitional Years in
   American Painting, 1885–1935*, 1963, no. 24.
The Brooklyn Museum, Brooklyn, New York, *American
   Painting: Selections from the Collection of Daniel and Rita
   Fraad*, June 9–September 20, 1964; Addison Gallery of
   American Art, Phillips Academy, Andover, Massachu-
   setts, October 10–November 8, 1964, no. 23 p. 31
   (illus.).

In contrast to the exuberance and gaiety of Potthast's trademark beach subjects, this nocturnal scene represents the contemplative side of an artist for whom evening shadows held great fascination.[1] The reflec-
tive tenor of the work and its division into general abstract patterns suggest the influence of Albert
Pinkham Ryder, whose canvases evoke similar romantic overtones. *A Summer's Night* probably dates to
the last few years of the artist's career, when he traveled to the Maine coast. These sojourns resulted in a
number of rock-and-sea studies, which, in their focus on the conjunction of clashing sea and rugged
shoreline, recall Winslow Homer's coastal views of Maine, dating some twenty years earlier.

   The colors are vivid: the moon casts a luminous green-and-purple glow on the figures and imparts a
pink cast to the rocks.[2] To accent the moon's reflection on the water, Potthast used slashing white impasto
brushstrokes. One critic, reluctant to embrace such strident colors, remarked in 1903 that Potthast's
paintings "reveal a positive and serious deterioration from his broad masculine style," decrying the "purple and pinks like so much sugar"[3] as major perpetrators of this decline. Employment of an intense color
scheme was a practice increasingly accepted over the course of Potthast's career, however, and later critics
were more sympathetic to the artist's palette.

1. Potthast's titles are problematic. A painting by the artist entitled *A Summer Night* was exhibited in Chicago and Cincinnati in
1908, but it is not the same painting as the one in the Fraad collection.
2. A nearly identical watercolor entitled *Enchanted* at the Hirshhorn Museum, Smithsonian Institution, is rendered in a similar
color scheme. See Abram Lerner, ed., *The Hirshhorn Museum and Sculpture Garden* (New York, 1974), fig. 236.
3. Anonymous review of an exhibition of Potthast's work at Katz Gallery, New York, *New York Mail*, March 26, 1903, Archives
of American Art, Smithsonian Institution, microfilm roll N738, frame 396.

24.

MAURICE B. PRENDERGAST (1859–1924)

Circus Band, c. 1895
monotype, 12¾ × 9⅜ in. (32.4 × 23.9 cm)

PROVENANCE
Jan Streep, New York and Amsterdam
[Ira Spanierman, New York, 1963]
[Davis Galleries, New York, 1963]

EXHIBITIONS
The Brooklyn Museum, Brooklyn, New York, *American Painting: Selections from the Collection of Daniel and Rita Fraad*, June 9–September 20, 1964; Addison Gallery of American Art, Phillips Academy, Andover, Massachu-setts, October 10–November 8, 1964, no. 35, p. 44 (illus.).
William Cooper Procter Art Center, Bard College, Annandale-on-Hudson, New York, *Maurice Prendergast: The Monotypes*, May 1–21, 1967, no. 56, p. 12.
Davis & Long Company, New York, *The Monotypes of Maurice Prendergast*, April 4–28, 1979, no. 41, p. 75 (illus.).

Born in Newfoundland and reared in Boston, Prendergast, who began his artistic career as an illustrator and calligrapher, and his brother, Charles, shared a common goal: to travel abroad to study European art. Their first trip overseas took place about 1886. However, it was during their second sojourn, from 1891 to 1894, that the popular Parisian Nouveau Cirque, a subject treated only in his monotypes, captured Prendergast's imagination, as it had the nineteenth-century French artists Henri Toulouse-Lautrec, Georges Seurat, and Edgar Degas.[1]

In *Circus Band*, a clown and a female figure in the costume of a bareback rider provide the musical accompaniment to a performance in the arena. A circle motif predominates, from the large central bass drum to the dot pattern of the performers' costumes, filling the surface of the monotype. Prendergast's use of these geometric shapes and his placement of a vertical post in the foreground create an ambiguous spatial arrangement seen also in the work of Toulouse-Lautrec. The flat, decorative, and rhythmic effect is characteristic of the French Nabis artists Pierre Bonnard and Edouard Vuillard, whose monotypes Prendergast admired.

The swirling, painterly style of *Circus Band* represents an inherent aspect of the monotype medium whereby an oil-based pigment applied to the surface of the printing plate can be easily manipulated. Prendergast would both push the paint around on the plate and scratch into the paint with the pointed end of a brush, thus combining the fluid technique of painting with the linearity of drawing. Once satisfied with the design, Prendergast transferred the pigment from the smooth copper plate to Japanese paper by rubbing the back side of the paper with a spoon.[2] Generally, the process yielded only one or two prints of each image.

Prendergast is regarded as a major figure in the history of the American monotype, both for the sheer quantity of his output (he produced approximately two hundred monotypes from about 1891 to 1902) and for the integral role that the monotype played in his *oeuvre*.[3]

1. The date for Prendergast's series of Nouveau Cirque monotypes is based on one dated work from the series, *Circus Scene with Horse* (Terra Museum of American Art, Evanston, Illinois).
2. Cecily Langdale, *The Monotypes of Maurice Prendergast* (New York, 1979), p. 8.
3. David W. Kiehl, "Monotypes in America in the Nineteenth and Early Twentieth Centuries," in *The Painterly Print: Monotypes from the Seventeenth to the Twentieth Century* (New York, 1980), pp. 43–44.

53

25.

MAURICE B. PRENDERGAST (1859–1924)

Venice, 1898
watercolor and graphite on paper, 18¼ × 15 in. (46.4 × 38.1 cm)
Inscribed l.l.: "Maurice B. Prendergast Venice 1898"
l.c.: "Fondamenta Del [illeg.]"

PROVENANCE
Mr. and Mrs. Curtis, 1940s (purchased in Paris)
S. G. Curtis, Jr., Los Angeles
[Armand Duvannes, Los Angeles]
[Maxwell Galleries, San Francisco, 1963]

EXHIBITIONS
Boston Watercolor Club, *Fifteenth Annual Exhibition*, Febru-
ary 28–March 15, 1902, no. 102 as *Fondamenta del Vino*.
The Brooklyn Museum, Brooklyn, New York, *American
Painting: Selections from the Collection of Daniel and Rita
Fraad*, June 9–September 20, 1964; Addison Gallery of
American Art, Phillips Academy, Andover, Massachu-
setts, October 10–November 8, 1964, no. 32, pp. 40–41
(illus.).
The Gallery of Modern Art, New York, *Major 19th and
20th Century Drawings*, January 19–February 21, 1965.
The Metropolitan Museum of Art, New York, *200 Years of
Watercolor Painting in America: An Exhibition Commemo-
rating the Centennial of the American Watercolor Society*,
December 8, 1966–January 29, 1967, no. 126, p. 22.

REFERENCES
Art News 61, no. 6 (October 1962): 63 (illus.).
Main Currents in Modern Thought 22, no. 3
(January–February 1966): cover (illus.).

In 1898 Prendergast embarked on his third trip abroad, spending the next eighteen months in France and Italy. Essentially self-taught, Prendergast utilized his European travel to broaden his exposure to the art of other cultures through sketching and making pilgrimages to museums and galleries. The rich historical and artistic heritage of Italy, and of Venice in particular, captivated him. Prendergast's numerous Venetian watercolors are devoted to the city's colorful street life and seem to appropriate the distinctive, shimmering luminosity of its many waterways.

Prendergast's ability to summarize the pageantry of Italian culture is generally attributed, in part, to his study of similarly crowded public scenes painted by the early Italian Renaissance masters. The vertical format and high horizon line of *Venice* create a cascading effect where figures, rendered in dashes of brilliant color, become increasingly distinct as they spill out of a relatively high focal point toward the foreground.

The view represented in this watercolor depicts the Riva del Ferro taken from near the bottom corner of the Rialto Bridge. A related watercolor, *The Grand Canal, Venice* (1898–1899, Terra Museum of American Art, Evanston, Illinois), depicts the view from the opposite side of the canal, at the other end of the Rialto Bridge.[1]

1. I am indebted to Carol Clark, Maurice and Charles Prendergast Executive Fellow, Williams College Museum of Art, Williamstown, Massachusetts, for her identification of these scenes and for sharing with me her extensive knowledge of Prendergast. The archives of the Prendergast systematic cataloguing project at Williams College contain a photograph of the watercolor in the Fraad collection inscribed on the verso in Prendergast's script: "Maurice B. Prendergast/Venice 1898."

26.

MAURICE B. PRENDERGAST (1859–1924)

Siena, 1898
watercolor and graphite on paper, 12¼ × 20⅛ in. (31.1 × 51.1 cm)
Inscribed l.r.: "Prendergast"

PROVENANCE
Lawrence Fleischman, Detroit
[Hirschl & Adler Galleries, New York, 1962]

EXHIBITIONS
University of Michigan, Museum of Art, Ann Arbor, *Mr. and Mrs. Lawrence Fleischman Collection of American Paintings*, November 15–December 6, 1953, no. 28, p. 11 (illus.).

The Detroit Institute of Arts, *Collection in Progress: Selections from the Lawrence and Barbara Fleischman Collection of American Art*, 1955, no. 28, pp. 24–25 (illus.).

Museo de Bellas Artes, Caracas, *Colección de arte norteamericano prestada por Lawrence A. Fleischman*, 1957, no. 32. Also traveled to Greece and Israel in 1958.

Milwaukee Art Center, *American Painting, 1760–1960: A Selection of 125 Paintings from the Collection of Mr. and Mrs. Lawrence A. Fleischman, Detroit*, March 3–April 3, 1960, p. 82 (illus.).

The Brooklyn Museum, Brooklyn, New York, *American Painting: Selections from the Collection of Daniel and Rita Fraad*, June 9–September 20, 1964; Addison Gallery of American Art, Phillips Academy, Andover, Massachusetts, October 10–November 8, 1964, no. 33, p. 42 (illus.).

In addition to Venice, Prendergast's 1898–1899 Italian sojourn included Florence, Rome, Capri, and Siena, where he spent two months. He executed perhaps as few as half a dozen watercolors of this Tuscan hill town. Most of the works in this series depict the central meeting area, the Piazza del Campo, although *Siena* represents a view taken at some distance from the heart of the city, whose skyline is dominated by the campanile of the Palazzo Pubblico.

The division of the image into distinct horizontal bands, a compositional device also employed by the artist in his Venetian watercolors, mimics the broad flat facades of Italian Renaissance architecture. In the foreground, a group of figures, primarily young girls, wear the billowing dresses that provide the decorative patterns Prendergast delighted in painting. Presaging a format developed in Prendergast's later oils (see cat. no. 29), these curvilinear forms contrast with the more static background, while the row of trees creates a bridge between the open quality of the park and the more contained building blocks of the town's architecture.

57

27.

MAURICE B. PRENDERGAST (1859–1924)

The Fountain at West Church, Boston, c. 1901
watercolor and graphite on paper, 12¾ × 22 in. (32.4 × 55.9 cm)
Inscribed l.c.: "Prendergast"

PROVENANCE
[Kraushaar Galleries, New York]
Mrs. Cornelius J. Sullivan, New York
(Sale, Parke-Bernet Galleries, New York, *Paintings, Drawings, Sculptures, Prints by Modern Artists . . . The Entire Collection of Mrs. Cornelius J. Sullivan,* December 6–7, 1939, no. 35, as *The Fountain*)
[Walker Galleries, New York, 1939]
Mrs. Walter Fletcher, 1962
[Hirschl & Adler Galleries, New York, 1962]

EXHIBITIONS
The Cleveland Museum of Art, Cleveland, Ohio, *Maurice Prendergast Memorial Exhibition,* 1926
IBM Gallery, New York, *Realism: An American Heritage,* January 14–February 1, 1963, no. 43, as *The Fountain,* n.p.
The Brooklyn Museum, Brooklyn, New York, *American Painting: Selections from the Collection of Daniel and Rita Fraad,* June 9–September 20, 1964; Addison Gallery of American Art, Phillips Academy, Andover, Massachusetts, October 10–November 8, 1964, no. 36, p. 45 (illus.).

Pembroke College Club of New York, Amel Gallery, *A Contemporary Art Exhibit from the private collections of Brown and Pembroke Alumni and Friends of the University,* April 18, 1965, n.p.
The Metropolitan Museum of Art, New York, 200 *Years of Watercolor Painting in America: An Exhibition Commemorating the Centennial of the American Watercolor Society,* December 8, 1966–January 29, 1967, no. 134, p. 24.

REFERENCES
Hirschl & Adler Galleries. *Selections from the Collection of Hirschl & Adler Galleries, Vol. IV* (New York, 1962–1963): no. 36, p. 25 (illus.), as *The Fountain—Gramercy Park.*
Kramer, Hilton. "In the Museums." *Art in America* 52, no. 2 (April 1964): 39 (illus.), as *The Fountain, Gramercy Park.*
Milliken, William Mathewson. "Maurice Prendergast, American Artist." *The Arts* 9, no. 4 (April 1926): 181 (illus.), 182, as *The Fountain, Boston.*
Rhys, Hedley Howell. *Maurice Prendergast, 1859–1924* (Cambridge, Mass., 1960), p. 95.

Increasing recognition through exhibitions of Prendergast's oils and watercolors in Boston and New York coincided with the artist's trip to Italy and continued upon his return. The Boston Watercolor Club Annual Exhibition in 1901 marked the first appearance of one in a series of works devoted to the courtyard in front of Boston's West Church, also known as Bartol Church, which, at the time Prendergast painted it, had been converted into a public library.[1] *The Fountain at West Church, Boston* and the four other known versions all depict clusters of figures surrounding a central fountain, one of the artist's favored pictorial formats.

Both the watercolor in the Fraad collecton and *Courtyard, West End Boston Library* (private collection) represent the view looking across the courtyard and away from the church. These two versions share a similar placement of figures and a very similar vantage point. The other three watercolors in this series actually represent the church itself: *Courtyard West End Library, Boston* (The Metropolitan Museum of Art, New York), *West Church, Boston* (Collection of Mr. and Mrs. Arthur G. Altschul, New York) and *West Church, Boston* (Museum of Fine Arts, Boston).

1. The inclusion of a work by this title in the 1901 exhibition, as well as stylistic factors, suggests a date of around 1901 for the watercolor in the Fraad collection. See Eleanor Green, *Maurice Prendergast* (College Park, Md., 1976), p. 103.

28.

MAURICE B. PRENDERGAST (1859–1924)

Picnicking Children—Central Park, c. 1901
watercolor and graphite on paper, 8¼ × 16¼ in. (21.0 × 26.0 cm)
Inscribed l.r.: "Prendergast"; and on verso: "Picnic 1895–97 (Boston Garden)"

PROVENANCE
Mrs. Charles Prendergast (sister-in-law of the artist)
[Davis Galleries, New York, 1962]
Owned jointly with Mr. and Mrs. Raymond J. Horowitz

EXHIBITIONS
The Brooklyn Museum, Brooklyn, New York, *American
Painting: Selections from the Collection of Daniel and Rita
Fraad*, June 9–September 20, 1964; Addison Gallery of
American Art, Phillips Academy, Andover, Massachu-
setts, October 10–November 8, 1964, no. 34, p. 43
(illus.).
The Metropolitan Museum of Art, New York, *American
Impressionist and Realist Paintings and Drawings from the
Collection of Mr. & Mrs. Raymond J. Horowitz*, April 19–
June 3, 1973, no. 30, pp. 102–103 (illus.), as *Picnic,
Boston Garden*.

REFERENCES
Stebbins, Theodore E., Jr. *American Master Drawings and
Watercolors: A History of Works on Paper from Colonial
Times to the Present* (New York, 1976), p. 248 (fig. 206),
as *Picnic: Boston Garden*.

Picnicking Children—Central Park, previously identified as a Boston Garden image, is linked in both style and subject matter to the period shortly after 1900, when Prendergast frequently visited New York and sketched Central Park in numerous variations.[1] One of the artist's favored subjects was the picnic, and in this version eight girls in an oval arrangement are gathered around a cloth laden with a picnic basket and food. Several of the figures closely correspond with those in the watercolor *The Picnic* (c. 1900, Museum of Art, Carnegie Institute, Pittsburgh), a more complex composition featuring as its central motif a group of girls similarly seated around an outdoor repast.[2] The presence of horses and riders in the Carnegie watercolor supports a Central Park locale for both it and *Picnicking Children*. They share with others in the series a flattening of the picture plane with a pronounced horizontal orientation and a row of repetitive forms in the upper register of the picture.

1. Dianne H. Pilgrim, *American Impressionist and Realist Paintings and Drawings from the Collection of Mr. & Mrs. Raymond J. Horowitz* (New York, 1973), no. 30 (illus. p. 102). Theodore E. Stebbins, Jr., *American Master Drawings and Watercolors: A History of Works on Paper from Colonial Times to the Present* (New York, 1976), p. 248 (illus., fig. 206).
2. I am grateful to Carol Clark for bringing the Carnegie watercolor to my attention.

61

29.

MAURICE B. PRENDERGAST (1859–1924)

Marblehead Rocks, c. 1915
oil on canvas, 20⅛ × 26⅛ in. (51.1 × 66.4 cm)
Inscribed l.r.: "Prendergast"

PROVENANCE
Mrs. Charles Prendergast (sister-in-law of the artist)
[Davis Galleries, New York, 1963]

EXHIBITIONS
Southern Vermont Art Center, Manchester, Vermont, *"The
Eight," Fifty-five Years Later*, June 22–July 7, 1960, no.
6, n.p.
The Brooklyn Museum, Brooklyn, New York, *American
Painting: Selections from the Collection of Daniel and Rita
Fraad*, June 9–September 20, 1964; Addison Gallery of
American Art, Phillips Academy, Andover, Massachu-
setts, October 10–November 8, 1964, no. 37, p. 46
(illus.).

Depicting a group of amorphous figures arranged in a friezelike pattern along a shore, *Marblehead Rocks*
is one in a series of related scenes executed by Prendergast after about 1914.[1] The many versions of this
theme illustrate the artist's prolonged experimentation with subtle variations of a composition devoted to
figures, trees, rocks, and boats dispersed across the picture plane.

Prendergast had an informed appreciation for art of many eras. In *Marblehead Rocks*, the flat, pat-
terned effect, created in part by the bold variegated lines ranging from black to purple and the slashes of
colorful pigment, recall sources as divergent as Byzantine mosaics and the European modernist modes
the artist enthusiastically noted on a trip to France in 1907.

In his assimilation of many aspects of the modernist style, especially the work of Cézanne, Matisse,
and the Nabis, Prendergast stands apart from his fellow members of The Eight, for whom subject matter
was a primary consideration. More ethereal in form than his other, earlier compositions of figures en-
gaged in leisure activities, the featureless subjects in *Marblehead Rocks* embody a timeless quality, and
location or context plays a secondary role to considerations of color, line, and form.

1. Prendergast spent many summers along the New England coast, which makes it difficult to pinpoint a date for this work.
Although a watercolor entitled *Marblehead Rocks* appeared in the 1913 Armory Show, it probably dates to the 1890s and is
stylistically more akin to Prendergast's earlier works than to his increasingly flat and decorative canvases as represented by this
painting in the Fraad collection. See Eleanor Green, *Maurice Prendergast* (College Park, Md., 1976), pp. 108–109.

63

30

ARTHUR B. DAVIES (1862–1928)

Nude in Landscape, c. 1908–1909
oil on canvas, 31¾ × 23¾ in. (80.7 × 60.3 cm)

PROVENANCE
Karl Ritz, Stockton, New Jersey
Mrs. Karl Ritz
[Albert Duveen, New York, 1966]

EXHIBITIONS
Southern Vermont Art Center, Manchester, Vermont, "*The Eight,*" *Fifty-five Years Later*, June 22–July 7, 1963, no. 1, n.p.

The Brooklyn Museum, Brooklyn, New York, *American Painting: Selections from the Collection of Daniel and Rita Fraad*, June 9–September 20, 1964; Addison Gallery of American Art, Phillips Academy, Andover, Massachusetts, October 10–November 8, 1964, no. 39, pp. 48–49 (illus.).

The primary organizer of the famed Armory Show, Arthur Bowen Davies was a native of Utica, New York. He worked as a draftsman in Mexico City from 1880 to 1882, studied at the Art Institute of Chicago in 1883, and then moved to New York in 1886 to work as an illustrator for magazines, such as *Century*. Trips abroad in 1895 and 1897 exposed him to contemporary European art and to classical antiquity, the frescoes at Pompeii, and the graceful women seen in the work of Botticelli and Piero di Cosimo.

Although Davies was a member of The Eight, his work was totally different from that of the majority of the group in mood and style. Instead, his idyllic landscapes and figure paintings are more in the tradition of works by Albert Pinkham Ryder, whom he met in 1900, and the Frenchman Pierre Puvis de Chavannes (1824–1898).[1] Davies greatly admired Ryder's depictions of mysterious, inner visions and Puvis' dreamy and muted paintings of monumental women in landscape settings. The influence of both of these artists can be seen in *Nude in Landscape*.

The graceful, attenuated woman in this painting, standing among the vaguely defined hills of the valley, dominates the subtly colored composition.[2] Although her facial features are not delineated, it has been proposed that the woman portrayed in Davies' paintings during this period is the dancer Edna Potter, with whom Davies began to live in 1905.[3] There is nothing lascivious in the demeanor of the nude. She is one of the pure and virtuous women presented as aloof, ethereal visions by many American artists (including Abbott Thayer and Thomas Wilmer Dewing) at the end of the nineteenth century.

The figure is shown in a dreamlike trance, similar to another of Davies' works of this time, *Dream* (or *Measure of Dreams*, c. 1908–1909, The Metropolitan Museum of Art, New York).[4] Although the themes of reverie and sleep were depicted by many artists—including academicians—at the turn of the

1. Davies would have known Puvis' work through his Boston Public Library murals (commissioned in 1890) and exhibitions of his work held in New York in 1888 and 1894.
2. Mahonri Sharp Young believes that the gently rolling hills in Davies' paintings are reminiscent of the Mohawk Valley in upstate New York, where the artist was raised. See Young's introduction to Joseph S. Czestochowski, *The Works of Arthur B. Davies* (Chicago, 1979), p. x.
3. Davies supported two families. He never divorced his wife, a doctor, who lived with their children in upstate New York. He and Potter lived in New York City under the names of Mr. and Mrs. David Owen. Brooks Wright, *The Artist and the Unicorn: The Lives of Arthur B. Davies* (New City, New York, 1978), p. 43, identifies Potter as the model for *The Great Mother* (The Corcoran Gallery of Art, Washington, D.C.) and *Do Reverence* (private collection, New York).
4. Joseph Czestochowski dates the painting c. 1908–1909 (Czestochowski to Linda Ayres, November 27 and December 19, 1984).

century, it was the Symbolists, such as Davies, who intensely explored the dream world in their art.[5] Davies was recognized as an American Symbolist when The Eight first exhibited and was compared to William Blake and Stephane Mallarmé.[6] Although colleagues and avant-garde collectors hailed Davies as a great artist, the majority of the public, accustomed to more literal scenes, found his work difficult to comprehend.

5. Charles C. Eldredge, *American Imagination and Symbolist Painting* (New York, 1979), p. 82.
6. *Philadelphia Press*, March 9, 1908, cited in Judith Zilczer, "The Eight on Tour, 1908–1909," *American Art Journal* 16, no. 3 (Summer 1984): 35.

31.

ROBERT HENRI (1865–1929)

Cumulus Clouds, East River, 1901–1902
oil on canvas, 25¼ × 31¾ in. (64.2 × 80.6 cm)
Inscribed l.r.: "Robert Henri"

PROVENANCE
Violet Organ (sister-in-law of the artist), until 1958
[Hirschl & Adler Galleries, New York, 1964]

EXHIBITIONS
Macbeth Gallery, New York, *Exhibition of Pictures by Robert Henri*, April 1–12, 1902.
Pennsylvania Academy of the Fine Arts, Philadelphia, *Exhibition of Landscapes and Portraits by Robert Henri*, November 1902; Pratt Institute, Brooklyn, New York, December 18, 1902–January 31, 1903, no. 20, n.p.
Hirschl & Adler Galleries, New York, *Robert Henri, 1865–1929, Fifty Paintings*, February 3–28, 1958, no. 12, cover (illus.).
Hirschl & Adler Galleries, New York, *The Hudson River:*

From New York to Albany, April 14–May 9, 1964, no. 24, n.p. (illus.).
The Brooklyn Museum, Brooklyn, New York, *American Painting: Selections from the Collection of Daniel and Rita Fraad*, June 9–September 20, 1964; Addison Gallery of American Art, Phillips Academy, Andover, Massachusetts, October 10–November 8, 1964, no. 74, p. 86 (illus.).
The Gallery of Modern Art, New York, *About New York, Night and Day, 1915–1965*, October 19–November 15, 1965, p. 17, as *East River*.

REFERENCES
Artist's Record Book A, no. 46.
Homer, William Innes. *Robert Henri and His Circle* (Ithaca, N.Y., 1969), pp. 229, 230 (illus., fig. 46).

Robert Henri, one of the most influential American artists and teachers of the early twentieth century, was born Robert Henry Cozad in Cincinnati, Ohio. After studying art at the Pennsylvania Academy of the Fine Arts and spending three years abroad in Paris, Brittany, and Venice, Henri taught at Emily Sartain's Philadelphia School of Design for Women (see cat. no. 8). In that city, he began to gather around him a group of artist-reporters—John Sloan, William Glackens, Everett Shinn, and George Luks—whom he encouraged to become painters. In 1900, Henri moved to New York, where he taught at the New York School of Art and continued his leadership of the group of progressive artists who rejected the style of impressionism being practiced by William Merritt Chase, John Twachtman, and Theodore Robinson. Instead of fashionable society portraiture or sun-drenched landscapes, Henri and his followers unsentimentally depicted urban life in a dark palette with rapid, broad brushwork. When their work began to be rejected for exhibition at the National Academy of Design, Henri organized an exhibition at the Macbeth Galleries in 1908, which gave birth to The Eight. The following year he opened his

own art school, where he taught George Bellows, Edward Hopper, Stuart Davis, and Guy Pène du Bois, among others.

Henri did some of his best work during his first years in New York, including a number of views of rivers, seen at different times of the day and under changing weather conditions. *Cumulus Clouds, East River* of 1901–1902 is one of these works.[1] Henri lived in a brownstone at 512 East 58th Street, on the banks of the East River, and his wife reported that "out of both front and back windows the river is fine—busy little boats hurrying by—and big white river steamers."[2]

1. Others include *Hudson River Docks* (1900–1902, Amherst College, Amherst, Massachusetts), *Blackwell's Island, East River* (1901, Whitney Museum of American Art, New York), *East River Embankment, Snow* (1900, Hirshhorn Museum and Sculpture Garden, Washington, D.C.), and *Summer Evening, North River* (or *Derricks on the North River*, 1902, Santa Barbara Museum of Art, Santa Barbara, California).
2. Quoted in William Innes Homer, *Robert Henri and His Circle* (Ithaca, N.Y., 1969), p. 99.

Cumulus Clouds, East River is a tonal painting of mood, an evocative depiction of activity on both shore and water along the city's commercial waterfront near the foot of 58th Street.[3] The time is sunset, with red, yellow, and gold reflections on the clouds and the building at right, but it is not brilliant pyrotechnics that we see. There is instead a murkiness, due in part to the clouds and possibly to industrial pollution as well.

Henri greatly admired James McNeill Whistler, and the painting's subject matter and overall color harmony call to mind Whistler's Thames series and nocturnes. The painting is also evocative of the poetry of Walt Whitman, whom Henri idolized, and Whitman's song of urban life.

Henri had begun to paint this type of cityscape in Paris in the 1890s, and it was reportedly at the urging of the New York dealer William Macbeth (after the French government bought Henri's *La Neige* in 1901) that Henri continued this theme in his new home of New York.[4] However, after 1902, Henri turned his attention from cityscapes to figure paintings and portraiture, for which he received more commissions.

3. Identified in the artist's Record Book A.
4. Homer, *Robert Henri and His Circle*, p. 108.

32.
ROBERT HENRI (1865–1929)

Sylvester—Smiling, 1914
oil on canvas, 24 × 20 in. (61.0 × 51.4 cm)
Inscribed l.r.: "Robert Henri"

PROVENANCE
Estate of the artist, until 1954
[Hirschl & Adler Galleries, New York, 1961]

EXHIBITIONS
Museum of History, Science, and Art, Los Angeles, *Paintings by Robert Henri*, September 14–30, 1914, no. 7, n.p., as *Sylvester*.
Macbeth Gallery, New York, Henri exhibition, November 1914 [?].
Pennsylvania Academy of the Fine Arts, Philadelphia, *110th Annual Exhibition*, February 7–March 28, 1915, no. 414, p. 48, as *Sylvester*.
Albright Art Gallery, Buffalo, *10th Annual Exhibition of Selected Paintings by American Artists*, May 22–August 30, 1915, no. 78, p. 14; City Art Museum, St. Louis, September 12, 1915, no. 76, p. 35, as *Sylvester*.
Fort Worth Museum of Art, Fort Worth, Texas, *Seventh Annual Exhibition of Selected Paintings*, January 4–29, 1916, no. 27, as *Sylvester*. Exhibition also traveled to the Austin Art League, Austin, Texas; San Antonio Art League, San Antonio, Texas; Galveston Art League, Galveston, Texas.
The Parthenon, Nashville, Tennessee, summer 1916.
Bedford and Brockton Public Library (Massachusetts), 1917.
Hirschl & Adler Galleries, New York, *Robert Henri: A Commemorative Exhibition*, March 31–April 30, 1954, no. 37.
Southern Vermont Art Center, Manchester, Vermont, "*The Eight,*" *Fifty-five Years Later*, June 22–July 7, 1963, no. 3, n.p.
The Brooklyn Museum, Brooklyn, New York, *American Painting: Selections from the Collection of Daniel and Rita Fraad*, June 9–September 20, 1964; Addison Gallery of American Art, Phillips Academy, Andover, Massachusetts, October 10–November 8, 1964, no. 27, p. 35 (illus.).

REFERENCES
Artist's Record Book I, no. 184.
Homer, William Innes. *Robert Henri and His Circle* (Ithaca, N.Y., 1969), p. 254.

One of Henri's former students, Alice Klauber of San Diego, urged him to spend the summer of 1914 in southern California. Plans were afoot there for a California Pacific Exposition, to be held the following

year, and Miss Klauber apparently asked for Henri's help in organizing the American art section. After a severe New York winter, Henri was more than ready for the California sun to "warm me up to the right heat of production,"[1] and he asked Miss Klauber to line up models for him: "Of course, I shall want to paint interesting people. I'm told you have them all the way [from] up to date class to the half breed and gipsy [*sic*]."[2]

Henri, with his second wife, Marjorie, and her sister, Violet, arrived in San Diego on June 16 and settled in a cottage in Richmond Court in La Jolla. The artist assisted in the planning of the 1915 exposition—which was to include George Bellows and six members of The Eight—and worked on a number of portraits of those "interesting people" he had mentioned earlier: Chicanos, American Indians, a Chinese vegetable man, and a black youngster named Sylvester, who sold newspapers at the train depot. In a 1915 article in *The Craftsman*, Henri explained his reaction to "my people," as he called them, "the people through whom dignity of life is manifest." He wrote: "My people may be old or young, rich or poor, I may speak their language or I may communicate with them only with gestures. But wherever I find them, the Indian at work in the white man's way, the Spanish gypsy moving back to the freedom of the hills, the little boy quiet and reticent before the stranger, my interest is awakened and my impulse immediately is to tell about them through my own language—drawing and painting in color."[3] Henri looked at each person with the hope of finding not only dignity (a word that recurs often in his text), but also "the humor, the humanity, the kindness, something of the order that will rescue the race and the nation."[4]

Children of the lower class had been a favorite subject for Henri (for example, *Eva Green* and *Cori and the Kitten* both of 1907), but *Sylvester—Smiling* ranks as one of his finest efforts in this genre. Executed with strong light-and-dark contrasts and broad, painterly brushstrokes, this work calls to mind Frans Hals, the seventeenth-century Dutch artist whose work Henri took his students to see in Holland in 1907. Sylvester's well-scrubbed mahogany skin and fresh white shirt are strongly lit and glisten against the plain dark background. One senses that Henri's brush moved quickly and surely, and, in fact, the artist's diary reveals that he could paint a full portrait in two hours and a portrait head in only forty-five minutes.[5]

Sylvester—Smiling, one of several portraits of the newsboy painted by Henri, is an unsentimental, spirited depiction of a child, in which the artist captured the essential dignity that he sought in all humans.[6]

1. Letter, Robert Henri to Alice Klauber, April 14, 1914, quoted in Martin E. Petersen, "Henri's California Visit," *Fine Arts Source Material Newsletter* 1, no. 2 (February 1971): 29.
2. Letter, Robert Henri to Alice Klauber, March 11, 1914, quoted in ibid., p. 29.
3. Robert Henri, "My People," *The Craftsman* 27, no. 5 (February 1915): 459.
4. Ibid., p. 467.
5. William Innes Homer, *Robert Henri and His Circle* (Ithaca, N.Y., 1969), p. 88.
6. Others include *The Failure of Sylvester*, showing him asleep in an armchair, no. 30 in Hirschl & Adler Galleries, *Robert Henri, 1865–1929, Fifty Paintings*, 1958; and *Sylvester*, no. 58 in the Metropolitan Museum's *Catalogue of a Memorial Exhibition of the Work of Robert Henri*, 1931.

33.
ROBERT HENRI (1865–1929)

The Sketchers in the Woods, c. 1918
pastel on paper, 12⅜ × 19½ in. (31.4 × 49.5 cm)
Inscribed l.r.: "R. Henri"

PROVENANCE
Violet Organ (sister-in-law of the artist), until 1954
[Hirschl & Adler Galleries, New York, 1958]

EXHIBITIONS
Milch Gallery, New York, *Annual Holiday Exhibition of
   Selected Paintings*, December 18, 1918–January 16,
   1919, no. 31, n.p., as *The Sketchers*.
Milch Gallery, New York, 1925.
Seattle Art Museum, February 6, 1944, no. 5 (typescript).
Hirschl & Adler Galleries, New York, *Robert Henri: A
   Commemorative Exhibition*, March 31–April 30, 1954,
   no. 42.
Hirschl & Adler Galleries, New York, *Robert Henri,
   1865–1929, Fifty Paintings*, February 3–28, 1958,
   no. 42.

The Brooklyn Museum, Brooklyn, New York, *American
   Painting: Selections from the Collection of Daniel and Rita
   Fraad*, June 9–September 20, 1964; Addison Gallery of
   American Art, Phillips Academy, Andover, Massachu-
   setts, October 10–November 8, 1964, no. 26, p. 34
   (illus.).
The Gallery of Modern Art, New York, *Major 19th and
   20th Century Drawings*, January 19–Feburary 21, 1965.

REFERENCES
Artist's Record Book K, no. 179.
Stebbins, Theodore E., Jr. *American Master Drawings and
   Watercolors: A History of Works on Paper from Colonial
   Times to the Present* (New York, 1976), p. 285 (illus.,
   fig. 245).

Robert Henri's first visit to Monhegan Island, off the coast of Maine, occurred in 1903, and he returned there in 1911 and 1918. Henri fell in love with the island and found it a "wonderful place to paint—so much in so small a place one can hardly believe it."[1] There was the ocean with its surf pounding on the rocks, the steep cliffs, and the village and its harbor. But a number of pastels dating from the last trip of 1918 (on which he was accompanied by George Bellows) indicate that it was the wild and dense pine forests that particularly captured his attention.[2]

For one accustomed to Henri's street scenes and his realistic portraits (see cat. nos. 31 and 32), the series of Monhegan pastels adds another dimension to the artist's *oeuvre*. Ted Stebbins believes these painterly pastels to be among Henri's best drawings and sees in them an impressionistic quality akin to Sargent.[3]

The Sketchers in the Woods is a fine example of the loosely rendered Monhegan works, with rich chalks laid down quickly on paper. It depicts two women in the hermetic world of the island forest. One is seated and one reclines (forming a stable, pyramidal composition) on gray barren rocks amid heavy green pine bowers. The artist identified the sitters in his records as "Ruth J." and Marjorie Organ Henri (his second wife), but he does not delineate the features of their faces in the pastel.[4] The subject is not so much the human form but the study of light and color in the outdoors.[5] Henri is interested in the way light filters through foliage, and it is apparent that his palette has brightened considerably since his early works (see cat. no. 31): blue, yellow, gold, and light green dance across the surface. Henri had become involved with the color theories of Hardesty S. Maratta in 1909 (see cat. no. 36), and this brighter palette can be attributed to that influence and to Henri's exposure to the high-keyed European works exhibited at the Armory Show in 1913.

1. William Innes Homer, *Robert Henri and His Circle* (Ithaca, N.Y., 1969), p. 112.
2. For instance, *Strollers' Rest* (1918, Collection of Raymond and Margaret Horowitz, New York) and the group of pastels that Henri exhibited in the *Eighteenth Annual Philadelphia Water Color Exhibition* at the Pennsylvania Academy of the Fine Arts (November 7–December 12, 1920). Bennard B. Perlman tells us that the virgin forest of Cathedral Woods was one of Henri's favorite spots on Monhegan (*Robert Henri, Painter* [Wilmington, Del., 1984], p. 113).
3. Theodore E. Stebbins, Jr., *American Master Drawings and Watercolors: A History of Works on Paper from Colonial Times to the Present* (New York, 1976), p. 285.
4. "Ruth J." was Ruth Jacobi, a former student of Henri. I am grateful to Bennard B. Perlman for this information.
5. In this sense, the Monhegan pastels represent a return to Henri's impressionistic work of the early 1890s (such as the scenes created in Avalon, New Jersey, in the summer of 1893). I am grateful to Mark Thistlethwaite for this observation.

34.
WILLIAM GLACKENS (1870–1938)
Untitled (Seated Woman), early 1900s
black chalk and black ink on parchment, 10⅝ × 9 in. (27.0 × 22.9 cm)

PROVENANCE
Estate of William Glackens
[Kraushaar Galleries, New York]
Gift of Mr. and Mrs. Raymond J. Horowitz, New York,
 1958

EXHIBITIONS
The Brooklyn Museum, Brooklyn, New York, *American Painting: Selections from the Collection of Daniel and Rita Fraad*, June 9–September 20, 1964; Addison Gallery of American Art, Phillips Academy, Andover, Massachusetts, October 10–November 8, 1964, no. 44, p. 54.

William Glackens, born in Philadelphia, worked for three of that city's newspapers, the *Record*, the *Press*, and the *Public Ledger*, as an artist-reporter and attended classes part-time at the Pennsylvania Academy of the Fine Arts. In 1895, he traveled to Belgium, Holland, and Paris, accompanying Robert Henri (with whom he shared a Philadelphia studio). Glackens settled in New York upon his return (the first of The Eight to move there) and supported himself by providing illustrations for various newspapers and magazines. This work trained his eyes to make rapid, accurate observations, and it is reported that wherever he went he carried a sketchbook to record any interesting image.[1]

Glackens' concise and straightforward drawings, such as *Seated Woman*, are the antithesis of the illustrations being done at the turn of the century by men like Charles Dana Gibson and Howard Chandler Christy. Instead of stylish and sentimental poses, Glackens endowed his subjects with expressive naturalism and, as early as 1899, he was recognized in America as a draftsman of unequaled skill.[2]

The woman depicted in this delicate and sensitive charcoal drawing leans forward with a sense of weariness and is evidence of Glackens' masterful draftsmanship. The work probably dates from the early 1900s.[3]

1. Janet Flint, *Drawings by William Glackens* (Washington, D.C., 1972), n.p.
2. Regina Armstrong, "Representative Young Illustrators," *Art Interchange* 43 (November 1899): 109, cited in William H. Gerdts, *American Impressionism* (New York, 1984), p. 278.
3. Telephone conversation with Richard Wattenmaker, December 13, 1984.

35.
WILLIAM GLACKENS (1870–1938)

Yellow Bath House and Sailboats, Bellport, L.I., c. 1916
oil on canvas, 18 × 24 in. (45.7 × 61.0 cm)
Inscribed l.l.: "W. Glackens"

PROVENANCE
[Kraushaar Galleries, New York]
Mr. and Mrs. Sidney Levyne, Baltimore, by 1949
[Hirschl & Adler Galleries, New York, 1962]

EXHIBITIONS
Kraushaar Galleries, New York, *Paintings and Drawings by William Glackens*, January 3–29, 1949, no. 20, n.p.
The Brooklyn Museum, Brooklyn, New York, *American*

Painting: Selections from the Collection of Daniel and Rita Fraad, June 9–September 20, 1964; Addison Gallery of American Art, Phillips Academy, Andover, Massachusetts, October 10–November 8, 1964, no. 43, pp. 52–53 (illus.).

REFERENCES
McIntyre, Robert G. *"The Eight," Fifty-five Years Later* (Manchester, Vt., 1963), n.p. (illus.).

Although William Glackens' early paintings—for which he is best known—display the dark palette of the Henri group, the influence of French art appears in his work as early as 1905, with the Manet-inspired *Chez Mouquin* (Art Institute of Chicago). A second trip to Europe in 1906 and subsequent visits during which he met Matisse and purchased pictures by Cézanne and Renoir for his friend Dr. Albert C. Barnes, the noted collector, had a profound impact on Glackens. These events reinforced Glackens' admiration for impressionist aesthetics, and his style began to change to one more akin to Ernest Lawson than to other members of The Eight, with whom he had formerly been aligned.

Although informal glimpses of everyday life remained Glackens' primary subject matter, the areas depicted switched increasingly from the lower class' streets in New York City to the leisure class' parks,

cafés, and beaches. Glackens' palette brightened as well, and his brushwork moved from bravura to broken lines. Bright outdoor light permeated his work.

One of the Glackens family's favorite resorts, Bellport, along the southern Long Island shore, served as the setting for a series of impressionistic paintings. Several scenes focus on the jetties and a particular bath house on South Bay.[1] *Yellow Bath House and Sailboats, Bellport, L.I.* of around 1916 belongs to this interesting group. The palette is charged with boldly juxtaposed and vibrant colors—mustard yellow, bright green, lavender, crimson, and pink. Even the sails, water, and sky reflect a spectrum of hues. The pigments are applied in an extraordinarily free and fresh manner, with broken brushwork (especially in the large sailboat) that forms two-dimensional patterns on the canvas. The figures on the pier and in the

1. Others from this series include *Bathers at Bellport*, c. 1920 (Phillips Collection, Washington, D.C.); *Bathing at Bellport, L.I.*, 1911 (The Brooklyn Museum, Brooklyn, New York); *Bathhouse, Bellport*, 1914 (private collection); *The Raft*, 1915 (Barnes Foundation, Merion, Pennsylvania); *Jetties at Bellport*, c. 1916 (Albright-Knox Art Gallery, Buffalo); *The Captain's Pier*, 1914 (private collection); and *Summer Day, Bellport, Long Island*, 1913 (John Russell Mitchell Foundation, Mt. Vernon, Illinois). Glackens also depicted the beaches at New London, Cape Cod, Blue Point, and St. Jean de Luz.

water appear as shimmering visions of reflected light and color with little volume or weight. The surface, with its hot, intense colors, feathery brushwork, and pulsating texture, reflects the artist's study of the work of Auguste Renoir, with which Glackens' later work is often compared.[2]

2. Albert E. Gallatin, "William Glackens," *American Magazine of Art* 7 (May 1916): 261–263, pointed out that the influence of Renoir on Glackens could be seen in his most recent work. Albert Barnes, in *The Art of Painting* (New York, 1928, first published in 1925), p. 361, considered Glackens, Lawson, and Prendergast the most important American Impressionists. On pp. 362–363, Barnes emphasized Glackens' relationship to Renoir. Both of the above are cited in William H. Gerdts, *American Impressionism* (New York, 1984), pp. 279 and 281, respectively.

36.
JOHN SLOAN (1871–1951)

Gray Day, Jersey Coast, 1911
oil on canvas, 21¾ × 25¾ in. (55.3 × 65.4 cm)
Inscribed l.r.: "John Sloan"

PROVENANCE
Estate of the artist (Helen Farr Sloan)
[Kraushaar Galleries, New York, 1963]

EXHIBITIONS
MacDowell Club, New York, 1914.
Kraushaar Galleries, New York, *Exhibition of Paintings by John Sloan*, April 11–30, 1921, no. 13, n.p., as *Coast, Gray Day.*
Wanamaker Galleries, Philadelphia, *John Sloan: Paintings, Etchings and Drawings*, January 8–29, 1940, no. 9, as *Gray Day New Jersey Coast.* (Although it appears that a catalogue of the Philadelphia show was not published, there is an annotated copy of the Sloan exhibition at the 1939 New York Wanamaker's show that indicates this painting was substituted for another when the show moved to Philadelphia.)

Southern Vermont Art Center, Manchester, Vermont, *"The Eight," Fifty-five Years Later*, June 22–July 7, 1963, no. 8, n.p.
The Brooklyn Museum, Brooklyn, New York, *American Painting: Selections from the Collection of Daniel and Rita Fraad*, June 9–September 20, 1964; Addison Gallery of American Art, Phillips Academy, Andover, Massachusetts, October 10–November 8, 1964, no. 41, p. 50 (illus.).

REFERENCES
Artist's Diary, September 4–11, 1911.
"Henri and Fellows at MacDowell Club." *American Art News* 12, no. 20 (February 21, 1914): 6.
Schwartz, Paul Waldo. "French Art Is Blooming Happily in Brooklyn." *International New York Times*, August 25, 1964 (illus.).

John Sloan, born in Loch Haven, Pennsylvania, was a classmate of William Glackens at Central High School in Philadelphia. Like Glackens, Sloan became a newspaper artist, beginning his career in 1892 with the *Philadelphia Inquirer*. During this time, he also attended Thomas Anshutz' classes at the Pennsylvania Academy of the Fine Arts. From 1895 to 1903, he worked at the *Philadelphia Press*, moving to New York in 1904, the last of his associates (Henri, Glackens, Shinn, and Luks) to settle there.

Through the encouragement of Robert Henri, with whom he had shared a Philadelphia studio, John Sloan became a painter. His views of New York streets and rooftops chronicle the everyday lives of city dwellers in the early twentieth century, but not all of his works have urban themes.

In 1911, around Labor Day, the artist and his wife, Dolly, visited a long-time friend, Edward Davis, at Belmar, New Jersey, a seashore town near Avon. Davis, the father of Stuart Davis, had been director of the art department at the *Inquirer* when Sloan worked there. Sloan's diary for September 5 reports that

he began an unusual painting that day at Belmar, "a rather large one of the sea, gray day, which seems right interesting for a first attempt at such a subject."[1] It was *Gray Day, Jersey Coast.*

Although it first appears that the men in the boat have come in from the offshore fish pound, Sloan's diary entry for September 8 reveals another scenario. Sloan and Stuart Davis, whom Helen Farr Sloan has identified as the standing figure on the boat,[2] found the worm-eaten remains of a shipwreck on the Avon shore and extracted copper from it. "Stuart and I worked like heroes and got two or three long keel

1. Diary of John Sloan, entry for September 5, 1911, quoted in Bruce St. John, ed., *John Sloan's New York Scene* (New York, 1965), p. 561.
2. Letter, Helen Farr Sloan to Antoinette Kraushaar, March 6, 1963.

bolts, solid copper, also some smaller copper spikes, bruised and banged up my tender feet and hands but I enjoyed this salvage very much."[3] The depiction of the salvage operation was no doubt completed in Sloan's New York studio.

The painting is a subtle, monochromatic work, with expansive horizontal bands of color—blue-gray overcast sky, gray sea with foamy white waves, and sandy beach—taking up most of the composition. The boat hulk, part of which is cropped by the canvas edge, is placed asymmetrically to the far left, with only a large basket in the sand at the right to counterbalance it. The figures are rapidly built up with dabs of color and little detail. The rich surface is comprised of broad, painterly brushstrokes, and the artist used a heavy, bold impasto for the sea. One senses vigor and restless movement throughout the work.

Sloan had begun, in 1909, to work with the color theories of Hardesty S. Maratta, and Helen Sloan reports that the Maratta palette was used in *Gray Day, Jersey Coast* to convey a "certain quality of mood and color orchestration."[4] The painting is indeed a sensitive and harmonious study of mood and atmosphere and remains a high-water mark in Sloan's *oeuvre*.

3. Sloan diary, entry for September 8, 1911, in St. John, *New York Scene*, pp. 561–562.
4. Letter, Helen Farr Sloan to Antoinette Kraushaar, March 6, 1963. Maratta, an artist and chemist, produced paints in tubes that were premixed to set color formulas. Robert Henri introduced Sloan and others to the Maratta pigments; George Bellows considered them the best in the world. For Sloan's comments on the Maratta palette, see St. John, *New York Scene*, especially pp. 318 and 514.

37.

JOHN SLOAN (1871–1951)

Woman on Couch, 1912
black crayon or charcoal on paper, 12½ × 8¾ in. (31.8 × 22.2 cm)
Inscribed l.l.: "–John Sloan–"
l.r. [by Helen Farr Sloan]: "c 1912 #706"

PROVENANCE
Estate of the artist (Helen Farr Sloan)
[Kraushaar Galleries, New York]
Gift of Raymond J. Horowitz, 1959

[Text for this entry is combined with that of
catalogue number 38, on page 80.]

38.

JOHN SLOAN (1871–1951)

The Black Hat, c. 1915
black crayon on paper, 13 × 19¼ in. (33.0 × 48.9 cm)
Inscribed l.l. [by Helen Farr Sloan]: "Black Hat—circa 1915"
l.r.: "John Sloan—/#1015" [number inscribed by Helen Farr Sloan]

PROVENANCE
[Kraushaar Galleries, New York]
Paul Magriel, New York, 1963

EXHIBITIONS
Norfolk Museum of Arts and Sciences, Norfolk, Virginia,
    American Drawing Annual XIX, January 12–Febru-
    ary 1, 1962, no. 81, n.p., owned by Paul Magriel.
Montclair Art Museum, Montclair, New Jersey, *American
    Drawings: A Selection from the Paul Magriel Collection*,
    March 11–25, 1962, no. 59, cover (illus.).
Rhode Island School of Design, Providence, *100
    American Drawings from the Collection of Paul Magriel*,
    September 16–October 14, 1962.

REFERENCES
Great Drawings of All Time (New York, 1972), 4: 1021
    (illus.).

John Sloan was a newspaper artist until 1903. After his move to New York in 1904, he worked as a free-lance illustrator for periodicals such as *Collier's* and *Century*. It was not until 1916, when he began to teach at the Art Students League (where Reginald Marsh and Peggy Bacon were among his students), that his principal income was no longer derived from illustration. Sloan's experience as an artist-reporter trained him to make quick and accurate observations about the objects and people he saw. He reportedly preferred to work from memory rather than from life, finishing his work rapidly once his model was gone.[1] He had experience drawing from the live model, however, first at the Charcoal Club in Phila-delphia in the 1890s and again, beginning in 1912, when he established a studio in New York.[2]

Woman on Couch is a sketchily drawn depiction of a woman napping. Sloan captured the essentials of the scene with a few quick strokes to indicate the couch, the woman's eyes and nose, and the relaxed body with her arms encircling her head.

The Black Hat is rendered in more detail. Although the sitter's hands and dress are rapidly sketched with an economy of line, Sloan has lingered over her face and, especially, on the dark, fashionable hat with its exuberant plumage.

1. Henry Adams, "John Sloan's *The Coffee Line*," *Carnegie Magazine* 57, no. 6 (November–December 1984): 21–22.
2. According to Lloyd Goodrich, in *John Sloan, 1871–1951* (New York, 1952), p. 7, members of the Charcoal Club sketched from the model two nights a week. David W. Scott and E. John Bullard, in *John Sloan, 1871–1951* (Washington, D.C., 1971), p. 23, state that Sloan began to paint regularly from the model with the establishment of his New York studio.

Black Hat - circa 1915

John Sloan

1015

39.
EVERETT SHINN (1876–1953)

Stage Scene, 1906
oil on canvas, 24 1/16 × 29 3/8 in. (61.1 × 74.6 cm)
Inscribed l.l.: "EVERETT SHINN / 1906"

PROVENANCE
The artist, until 1946
The Lotos Club, New York, 1946
[Hammer Gallery, New York, 1964]

EXHIBITIONS
Southern Vermont Art Center, Manchester, Vermont, *"The
Eight," Fifty-five Years Later*, June 22–July 7, 1963,
no. 7, n.p.
The Brooklyn Museum, Brooklyn, New York, *American
Painting: Selections from the Collection of Daniel and Rita
Fraad*, June 9–September 20, 1964; Addison Gallery of
American Art, Phillips Academy, Andover, Massachu-
setts, October 10–November 8, 1964, no. 45, p. 55
(illus.).

Everett Shinn, the youngest of the Philadelphia artist-reporters who banded together with Robert Henri, was born in Woodstown, New Jersey. After studying mechanical drawing and engineering in Phila-delphia, he took classes in 1893 at the Pennsylvania Academy of the Fine Arts and began to work at the *Philadelphia Press* and subsequently at the *Ledger* and *Inquirer*. In 1897 he moved to New York to con-tinue his career as an illustrator (see cat. no. 40).

In New York, Everett Shinn showed a keen interest in the theater (a taste perhaps developed at the amateur theatricals held at Henri's Philadelphia studio). His friends included the actress Julia Marlowe and the playwright Clyde Fitch. Shinn built a 55-seat theater in his home at 112 Waverly Place, complete with proscenium stage and crimson curtains. There he presented plays that he wrote, casted, and di-rected, and for which he built stage sets. The performances of his "Waverly Street Players" (which in-cluded William Glackens and his wife), were reviewed by the *New York Times*.[1]

Shinn's fascination with the stage is reflected in his paintings, from works dating from the early part of the twentieth century, such as *Stage Scene* of 1906, to material he painted as late as the 1930s.[2] These theatrical works are in direct contrast to the unglamorous, often gritty scenes depicted by other members of the Ashcan School, and they are influenced by the French painters of the stage, Edgar Degas and Henri Toulouse-Lautrec, whose work Shinn saw on a trip to France at the turn of the century.

1. Edith DeShazo, *Everett Shinn, 1876–1953: A Figure in His Time* (New York, 1974), p. 71. Shinn's brother, Warren, ran dances at the Opera House in Woodstown, New Jersey, and Everett made posters for him.
2. Other early stage scenes include *The Orchestra Pit, Old Proctor's Fifth Avenue Theatre*, c. 1906–1907 (Collection of Arthur Altschul, New York); *Theatre Box*, 1906 (Albright-Knox Art Gallery, Buffalo); *Theater*, 1908 (Whitney Museum of American Art, New York); and *Matinee, Outdoor Stage, Paris*, a pastel of 1902 (Collection of Raymond and Margaret Horowitz, New York).

In *Stage Scene*, a subtly colored painting, we see that the dramatic, artificial lighting of the stage particularly attracted Shinn, as did the costumes and the fashionable audience. *Stage Scene* depicts two coquettish young actresses bowing to the audience in an ornate theater setting. The women are shown against a backdrop of a painterly stage set suggestive of a balcony or terrace. Their faces, particularly their noses and chins, are lit from below by harsh footlights. The viewer's perspective is from a higher row, looking down onto the orchestra pit, which is indicated by the elegant curve of the neck of a stringed bass and the glowing white sheets of music in the darkness. In a box adjacent to the musicians sits a group of fashionably dressed women, one of whom looks out to stare at the viewer. George Bellows would use this same motif of a figure turning to look at the viewer in several of his boxing pictures, including the 1907 *Knock Out* (see cat. no. 44).

Shinn presented *Stage Scene* to New York's Lotos Club in 1946 when he became a member.

40.

EVERETT SHINN (1876–1953)

Out of a Job—News of the Unemployed, 1908
wash, black crayon, and graphite on paper, 13⅞ × 27 ¹⁵⁄₁₆ in. (35.2 × 70.8 cm)
Inscribed l.r.: "EVERETT SHINN / 1908."

PROVENANCE
Mrs. Ethel Parsons Paullin
[Kraushaar Galleries, New York, 1964]

EXHIBITIONS
The Gallery of Modern Art, New York, *Major 19th and
    20th Century Drawings*, January 19–February 21, 1965.

REFERENCES
*American Manners & Morals: A Picture History of How We
    Behaved and Misbehaved* (New York, 1969), p. 386
    (illus.).
Davidson, Marshall B. *The Drawing of America: Eyewitness
    to History* (New York, 1983), p. 212 (illus., fig. 261).
Ruhl, Arthur. "Out of a Job—News of the Unemployed."
    Collier's (April 18, 1908), p. 19.

Everett Shinn was an extremely talented draftsman. His skills were innate but were honed through positions at a number of leading newspapers and periodicals. It was a job at the *New York World* that brought him to that city in 1897, and he also worked for the art departments of the *Journal* and the *Herald*. He later began to contribute illustrations of city life to popular magazines, such as *Harper's* (both weekly and monthly) and *Scribner's*, which provided a better income than newspaper work.

Out of a Job—News of the Unemployed appeared in the April 18, 1908, issue of *Collier's* and illustrated an article of the same title written by Arthur Ruhl. The story was the first of a three-part series, "Describing the Case of the Idle Workman." Ruhl's text dealt with the results of an economic panic, and the "wrenching and squeezing and tearing of the strength and hope and faith and opportunity and fighting spirit of hundreds of thousands of men and women."[1] He described the block-long line of people who gathered at night for free sandwiches and coffee in Madison Square Garden and the bread line—twice as long as in other years—on Broadway near Grace Church.

It is the dispirited men in the bread line at 10th and Broadway that Shinn depicts in this drawing. The men stand huddled, their hands in their pockets, in the chill of a rainy night. Their coats catch the rays of the streetlight, and the wet pavement reflects their dark forms in the silent queue. Shinn has captured, in rich black crayon, the variety of people, their faces revealing a range of expressions. He shows us the vagrants, with their look of resignation, and the businessmen (like the two at the right who glance warily at the left group) to whom this situation is frighteningly new.

1. Arthur Ruhl, "Out of a Job—News of the Unemployed," *Collier's* (April 18, 1908), pp. 19–20. Ruhl estimated that in New York, in February and March 1908, there were 150,000–200,000 unemployed people.

85

41.

GEORGE LUKS (1866–1933)

The Cabby (New York Cabby), 1921
oil on canvas, 29 ½ × 24 ½ in. (74.9 × 62.2 cm)
Inscribed l.r.: "George Luks—"

PROVENANCE

Estate of the artist
(Sale, Parke-Bernet Galleries, New York, *Paintings, Watercolors and Drawings by George B. Luks, Property of the Estate of the Late George B. Luks*, April 5, 1950, no. 68, illus., as *New York Cabby*)
[Babcock and Milch Galleries, New York]
Joseph Katz, Baltimore
[Hirschl & Adler Galleries, New York, 1959]

EXHIBITIONS

Kraushaar Galleries, New York, *Recent Paintings & Water Colors by George Luks*, January 12–31, 1922, no. 10, n.p., as *New York Cabby*.
The Cleveland Museum of Art, Cleveland, Ohio, *Twelfth Exhibition of Contemporary American Oil Paintings*, June 10–July 10, 1932, no catalogue.

Frank K. M. Rehn Galleries, New York, *Paintings and Drawings by George Luks*, March 19–April 7, 1934, no. 8, n.p.
[Possibly] Whitney Museum of American Art, New York, 1937.
Hirschl & Adler Galleries, New York, *The Portrait in American Art*, April 13–May 9, 1959, no. 40.
Southern Vermont Art Center, Manchester, Vermont, *"The Eight," Fifty-five Years Later*, June 22–July 7, 1963, no. 5, n.p.
The Brooklyn Museum, Brooklyn, New York, *American Painting: Selections from the Collection of Daniel and Rita Fraad*, June 9–September 20, 1964; Addison Gallery of American Art, Phillips Academy, Andover, Massachusetts, October 10–November 8, 1964, no. 47, p. 57 (illus.).

REFERENCES

Sportsman (December 1933), cover (illus.).

George Luks was born in Williamsport, Pennsylvania, the son of amateur painters, and studied under Thomas Anshutz at the Pennsylvania Academy in 1884. He traveled to Düsseldorf, Munich, Paris, and London to study the works of Hals, Rembrandt, Velásquez, and Goya and then returned to Philadelphia, where, in 1894, he joined the art department of the *Philadelphia Press*. There he continued his association with several men he had met while a student at the Academy, who later banded together to form The Eight.

After going to Cuba in late 1895 as a war correspondent for the *Philadelphia Evening Bulletin*, Luks moved to New York in 1896 and became a cartoonist for the *New York World*. Newspaper work, requiring keen observation of people and details and rapid sketching served Luks well in his paintings, and *The Cabby* (*New York Cabby*) of 1921 is a fine example of the people that Luks brought to life on canvas. By the time this work was created, Luks had left newspaper work to paint and to teach at the Art Students League (he would later found his own school), but he still was an incisive commentator on the life and activities of the common people. His sitters are vibrant and colorful characters.

The solid figure of the cabby, in coal black top hat and overcoat, is placed against a reddish-brown background. Luks filled up most of the space with the figure and placed him close to the picture plane, conveying a sense of immediacy and capturing an unguarded expression, something Luks called "edge."[1] Raising his brown buggy whip, the old man seems to be giving a command to his horses. His thickly painted face, the focal point of the composition, comes alive with nose, cheeks, and lips reddened by the cold weather.

Typical of work by The Eight in its low-keyed palette, bravura handling of the brush, and urban subject matter, *The Cabby* is not a caricature but a compellingly bold portrayal of a robust, hard-working

1. Munson-Williams-Proctor Institute, *George Luks, 1866–1933* (Utica, N.Y., 1973), p. 18.

man. Like the seventeenth-century Dutch artist Frans Hals, with whom he often compared himself, Luks captured his sitters in a style of powerful, sometimes brutal, realism. Everett Shinn commented: "He slices like a surgeon down to deep internals and sews in a gland that distributes vitality and pulsates close in artificial respiration. Somehow the thing goes on and lives by its own witchery, that something that is done apart from brush and paint."[2]

      Luks must have been particularly fascinated with the theme of the cab driver, for he painted it several times. One of his early efforts was an 1889 oil entitled *London Cabby* (The Memorial Art Gallery, University of Rochester), showing a rotund man in bowler hat and boutonnière. *Cabby at the Plaza*, a smaller (12 × 10 inches) version of the painting in the Fraad collection, is in the New Britain Museum of American Art, and various other studies of cabbies exist.[3]

2. "Everett Shinn on George Luks: An unpublished Memoir," *Archives of American Art Journal* 6, no. 6 (1966): 9.
3. A small study for the Fraads' painting, *The Cabbie* (oil on panel, 9¾ × 8¼ inches), is illustrated in *Selections from the Collection of Hirschl & Adler Galleries, Vol. V* (New York, 1963–1964), no. 32. The University of Georgia owns Luks' *Jerry, the Plaza Cabbie* (oil on canvas, 20 × 16 inches), which depicts a man with white hair and moustache. There are two cabby paintings (both oil on board) listed in Alfredo Valente Gallery, New York, *The Ashcan School*, November 7–December 7, 1961, nos. 12 (illus.) and 13. Mr. and Mrs. William M. Fuller (Fort Worth, Texas) own *The Cabby* (oil on wood panel, 9¾ × 8¼ inches) and *Study for The Cabby* (charcoal on paper, 6¾ × 4¼ inches).

42.

CHARLES WEBSTER HAWTHORNE (1872–1930)

The Morning Coffee, c. 1918
oil on canvas, 30 × 30 in. (76.2 × 76.2 cm)
Inscribed l.l.: "C. W. Hawthorne"

PROVENANCE
Joseph Hawthorne, Toledo (son of the artist)
[Babcock Galleries, New York, 1957]

EXHIBITIONS
Provincetown Art Association, Provincetown, Massachusetts, *Special Charles W. Hawthorne Memorial Exhibition*, in *First 1952 Exhibition*, June 29–July 27, 1952, and *Second 1952 Exhibition*, August 3–September 1, 1952, no. 52, n.p.
Des Moines Art Center, Iowa, *Realism in Painting and Sculpture*, June 1953, n.p.

The Toledo Museum of Art, *Chase and Hawthorne, Two American Teachers*, December 1–29, 1957, no catalogue.
The Chrysler Art Museum, Provincetown, Massachusetts, *Hawthorne Retrospective*, June 16–September 17, 1961, no. 85, p. 64 (illus.).
The Brooklyn Museum, Brooklyn, New York, *American Painting: Selections from the Collection of Daniel and Rita Fraad*, June 9–September 20, 1964; Addison Gallery of American Art, Phillips Academy, Andover, Massachusetts, October 10–November 8, 1964, no. 25, p. 33 (illus.).

Charles Hawthorne, though born in Illinois, grew up in Maine, the son of a sea captain. After taking art classes at night in New York and working on the docks and in a stained-glass factory during the day, Hawthorne had the opportunity to study in 1896 with William Merritt Chase at Chase's summer school at Shinnecock, Long Island. He later became Chase's assistant at both Shinnecock and the master's school in New York City. After an 1898 trip to Holland to study Frans Hals and to paint that country's fishing folk and villagers, Hawthorne returned to the United States to establish his own summer school,

the Cape Cod School of Art in Provincetown, Massachusetts, where he became a well-known teacher in his own right.

In Provincetown, an isolated fishing village, Hawthorne taught and painted for over three decades, and it is his portrayals of Provincetown residents—old New Englanders and Portuguese immigrants—for which he is best known today. One of his finest portraits is *The Morning Coffee* of about 1918.

The painting uses the square format favored by Hawthorne and depicts an elderly Yankee, "Old

Ben," in a gray workshirt and purplish-blue vest seated against a dark gray background.[1] The sitter's hand, which has known hard work, stirs coffee in a white cup and saucer. Even more worn and weary is the expression on the man's face, his watery eyes circled with red, his hair and moustache turning gray. Hawthorne's son, Joseph, reported that his father began a portrait by painting the eyes, and it is the riveting gaze of the sitter that makes the image so compelling.[2] From Hals and from Chase, Hawthorne learned robust brushwork and how to contrast dramatically strong lights and darks. From the Venetian artists, whom Hawthorne studied during a two-year stay in Italy in the early part of the century, he learned bold and deep coloration and monumental forms. All of these come together in *The Morning Coffee.*

A straightforward character study of a common man, *The Morning Coffee* relates to other works in the exhibition, notably George Luks' *The Cabby* (1921, cat. no. 41) and Robert Henri's *Sylvester—Smiling* (1914, cat. no. 32).

1. Joseph Hawthorne reports that the records for his father's paintings list this work as *The Coffee Drinker* and, alternatively, as *Old Ben*, since that was the name of the sitter, a Provincetown resident (letter to Linda Ayres, January 4, 1985).
2. The Chrysler Art Museum, *Hawthorne Retrospective* (Provincetown, Mass., 1961), p. 9.

43.

GEORGE BELLOWS (1882–1925)

Kids, 1906
oil on canvas, 32 × 42 in. (81.2 × 106.6 cm)
Inscribed l.l.: "Geo. Bellows"

PROVENANCE
Estate of the artist
Emma S. Bellows (wife of the artist)
Estate of Emma S. Bellows
[H. V. Allison & Company, New York, 1964]

EXHIBITIONS
Society of American Artists, Fine Arts Galleries, New York, *Twenty-Eighth Annual Exhibition*, March 17–April 22, 1906, no. 27, p. 26.
H. V. Allison & Company, New York, *George Bellows*, May 7–29, 1964, no. 1, cover (illus.).
The Brooklyn Museum, Brooklyn, New York, *American Painting: Selections from the Collection of Daniel and Rita Fraad*, June 9–September 20, 1964; Addison Gallery of American Art, Phillips Academy, Andover, Massachu-

setts, October 10–November 8, 1964, no. 75, p. 87 (illus.).
The Gallery of Modern Art, New York, *George Bellows, Paintings, Drawings, Lithographs*, March 15–May 1, 1966, no. 2, pp. 9, 17 (illus.).
Whitney Museum of American Art, New York, *The Painter's America: Urban and Rural Life, 1810–1910*, September 18–November 10, 1974, pp. 129, 152 (illus.).

REFERENCES
Artist's Record Book A, p. 14.
The Brooklyn Museum. *Summer Bulletin*, 1964.
Homer, William Innes. *Robert Henri and His Circle* (Ithaca, N.Y., 1969), pp. 199, 200 (illus., fig. 33).
Morgan, Charles H. *George Bellows, Painter of America* (New York, 1965), pp. 52, 69.

George Bellows was born in Columbus, Ohio, and attended Ohio State University. In 1904, he moved to New York and enrolled in the New York School of Art, where he studied with Robert Henri and became the older artist's close friend. His early work is close in spirit and style to that of Henri and exhibits the Ashcan School's dark palette, energetic, broad brushwork, and direct observation of commonplace subjects. Henri deemed anything worthy of painting, as long as it dealt with life, and the New York realists delighted in depicting the inhabitants of that city's poorer districts.

Perhaps inspired by George Luks' 1905 canvas of two joyful immigrant girls dancing (*The Spielers,*

Addison Gallery of American Art, Phillips Academy, Andover, Massachusetts), Bellows in 1906 painted *Kids*, an exuberant scene portraying poor, immigrant children playing in an alley.[1] The painting, executed in broad, painterly strokes is fairly monochromatic, but Bellows included some exquisite passages of color, such as the salmon pink shirt on the lanky girl near the center of the canvas and the cream-colored carriage to the left. As Charles Morgan has noted, the composition is based on William Hogarth's "line of beauty," with an S-curve down the center.[2] The awkwardly dressed children are in groups of threes and fours—some huddled in conversation, others playing with uninhibited glee, and a few standing shyly off to the side. Although Bellows shows us only a few of their faces, those faces are caricatured in a way that recalls the work of the nineteenth-century French artist Honoré Daumier, whose prints Henri urged his students to study.[3]

Bellows' first major canvas was praised by the critics when it was shown in 1906 at the final exhibi-

1. Although Bellows, in his Record Book, dated *Kids* April 1906, the painting was exhibited at the Society of American Artists the previous month.
2. Charles H. Morgan, *George Bellows, Painter of America* (New York, 1965), p. 52.
3. Francine Tyler, "The Impact of Daumier's Graphics on American Artists: c. 1863–1923," *Print Review* 11 (1980): 119.

tion of the Society of American Artists, and perhaps this success encouraged Bellows to paint other scenes of city children in this period, including *River Rats* (1906, Mr. Everett Reese, Columbus, Ohio) and *Forty-Two Kids* (1907, The Corcoran Gallery of Art, Washington).

44.

GEORGE BELLOWS (1882–1925)

The Knock Out, July 1907
pastel and India ink on paper, 21 × 27½ in. (53.3 × 69.9 cm)
Inscribed u.r.: "Bellows."; and on verso in pencil: "GEO BELLOWS / 1947
BROADWAY / N.Y. / 'A KNOCK OUT'"

PROVENANCE
The artist
Joseph B. Thomas, Esq., New York, by 1911
Mrs. Charles W. Clark, San Mateo, California, 1916
The Rosenbach Company, Philadelphia, ?–1952
The Philip H. and A. S. W. Rosenbach Foundation,
Philadelphia, 1952–1976
[Herring Brothers, New York, 1976]
[Davis & Long Company, New York, 1976]

EXHIBITIONS
Fellowship of the Pennsylvania Academy of the Fine Arts,
Philadelphia, *Eighth Annual Exhibition*, October 28–
November 17, 1907.
Exhibition of 16 at 42nd Street Gallery, New York, 1907.
American Water Color Society, New York, *Forty-first An-
nual Exhibition*, April 30–May 24, 1908, no. 350, p. 34.
Chicago Water Color Club, 1909.
Exhibition of Independent Artists, New York, April 1–27,
1910, no. 185, as *A Knockout*.
Gallery of Fine Arts and Art Association of Columbus, Ohio
(held at Columbus Public Library), *Exhibition of Paint-
ings by American Artists*, January 1911, no. 70, as *A
Knock-out*, lent by Joseph B. Thomas, Esq.
Powell Art Gallery, New York, 1912.
City Club, 1912.

Panama Pacific Exhibition, San Francisco, 1916, according
to the Record Book (but not listed in the exhibition
catalogue).
National Gallery of Art, Washington, D.C., *George Bellows:
A Retrospective Exhibition*, January 19–February 24,
1957, no. 73, pp. 24, 110 (illus.), lent by The Philip H.
and A. S. W. Rosenbach Foundation.
Delaware Art Center, Wilmington, *The Fiftieth Anniversary
of the Exhibition of Independent Artists in 1910*,
January 9–February 21, 1960, no. 5, lent by The
Philip H. and A. S. W. Rosenbach Foundation.
Isaac Delgado Museum, New Orleans Museum of Art,
World of Art in 1910, November 15–December 31, 1960,
no number, lent by The Philip H. and A. S. W.
Rosenbach Foundation.
National Gallery of Art, Washington, D.C., *Bellows: The
Boxing Pictures*, September 5, 1982–January 2, 1983,
pp. 47 (illus., pl. 6), 51 (illus., fig. 52), 52, 53, 83.

REFERENCES
Artist's Record Book A, p. 38.
Braider, Donald. *George Bellows and the Ashcan School of
Painting* (New York, 1971), pp. 42, 68–69.
Morgan, Charles H. *George Bellows, Painter of America*
(New York, 1965), p. 76, 77, 128, 129.

Bellows is best remembered as a painter of the boxing ring and, indeed, pugilism was a recurring theme in his career.[1] The subject was not a new one in American art. Thomas Eakins had portrayed boxers in the late 1890s (for example, *Between Rounds* of 1899, Philadelphia Museum of Art), William Glackens produced *The Boxing Match* in 1906 (Collection of Arthur Altschul, New York), and, relatedly, George Luks depicted *Wrestlers* (Museum of Fine Arts, Boston) with stark brutality in 1905.

It is not surprising that Bellows was drawn to boxing as subject matter, for he was a talented athlete, having been invited to join the Cincinnati Reds prior to his move to New York. But his interest in this

1. See E. A. Carmean, Jr., John Wilmerding, Linda Ayres, and Deborah Chotner, *Bellows: The Boxing Pictures* (Washington, D.C., 1982). *The Knock Out* is discussed in detail on pp. 51–53.

particular sport was probably reinforced by the proximity of his studio to one of New York's boxing clubs. In September 1906, Bellows and two friends, Ed Keefe and Fred Cornell, moved to the Lincoln Arcade at 1947 Broadway (at the corner of 65th Street). Across Lincoln Square at 66th Street was Tom Sharkey's Athletic Club, where Sharkey, a former boxer, set up a ring in the back room (boxing was illegal in New York at this time). Bellows' first visit to Sharkey's occurred when Moses King, the light-weight champion of Connecticut and a friend of Ed Keefe, fought a match there. The result of this visit is the large and powerful pastel, *The Knock Out*, of 1907. It is Bellows' first boxing image and one of the finest drawings this consummate draftsman ever created.

The pastel is not a sketch, but a highly finished work rendered in Bellows' bold and direct style. It depicts the dramatic climax of a fight in Sharkey's crowded, hot, and smoky back room in which the referee struggles to restrain the victor from continuing to beat the collapsed loser. As the frenzied crowd begins to climb into the ring, a caricatured face (like one seen in the work of Goya or Daumier) turns to look at the viewer. Bellows does not show us the faces of any of the principal protagonists; his emphasis instead is on the anatomical structure of their bodies.

The drawing, executed with unhesitant painterly strokes, primarily monochromatic tones of brown, gray, and black, exudes an air of spontaneity since the viewer is placed in the audience at ringside. This sort of bold realism in Bellows' work was controversial, and when *The Knock Out* was exhibited in Columbus, Ohio, in 1911 it was shown only to adult males in a locked and guarded room.[2]

In 1921, Bellows used the same composition seen in this pastel as the basis for two lithographs, both entitled *A Knockout*.[3]

2. Donald Braider, *George Bellows and the Ashcan School of Painting* (New York, 1971), p. 68.
3. These two prints are included in the complete set of Bellows' boxing lithographs owned by Rita and Daniel Fraad.

45.
GEORGE BELLOWS (1882–1925)

Shore House, January 1911
oil on canvas, 40 × 42 in. (101.6 × 106.7 cm)
Inscribed l.l.: "Geo Bellows."

PROVENANCE
Estate of the artist
Emma S. Bellows (wife of the artist)
Estate of Emma S. Bellows
[H. V. Allison and Company, New York]
C. Ruxton Love, Jr., New York, 1956
Estate of C. Ruxton Love, Jr., 1971
[Hirschl & Adler Galleries, New York, 1972]

EXHIBITIONS
National Arts Club, 1911, traveling exhibition of paintings by life members, to Worcester, Massachusetts; Detroit Museum of Art, February 1–March 10, 1911; Rhode Island School of Design, Providence, April 21–May 12, 1911; and Marshall Field, Chicago (dates available for Detroit and Providence venues only).
Madison Gallery, New York, *George Bellows*, January–February 3, 1911.
MacDowell Club, New York, 1912.
Minnesota State Art Society, 1912.
Texas State Fair, Dallas, 1912.
Curtis, New Haven, 1913.
Art Institute of Chicago, *Paintings by George Bellows*, December 10, 1914–January 3, 1915.
San Francisco, 1915.
Detroit Museum of Art, *Exhibition of Paintings by George Bellows*, January 6–29, 1915, no. 9, n.p.
Museum of History, Science, and Art, Los Angeles, *Paintings by George Bellows, N.A.*, February 7–28, 1915.

Minneapolis Institute of Arts, *Paintings by Lester D. Boronda; Paintings by George Bellows*, May 4–31, 1915.
Hackley Art Gallery, Muskegon, Michigan, *Exhibition of Oil Paintings by George Bellows*, June 9–August 15, 1915.
Worcester Art Museum, Massachusetts, *Exhibition of Paintings by George Bellows, New York City*, September 5–26, 1915, no. 14, n.p.
The Cincinnati Art Museum, *Special Exhibition of Paintings by Mr. George Bellows*, October 1915.
Art Club, Boston, 1916.
Columbus Gallery of Fine Arts, Columbus, Ohio, *Thirty-six Paintings by George Bellows*, October 3–November 6, 1940.
H. V. Allison & Company, New York, *Paintings by George Bellows*, October 19–November 21, 1942, n.p.
Art Institute of Chicago, *George Bellows: Paintings, Drawings, and Prints*, January 31–March 10, 1946, no. 12, pp. 22 (illus.), 39.
National Gallery of Art, Washington, D.C., *George Bellows: A Retrospective Exhibition*, January 19–February 24, 1957, no. 21, pp. 17, 57 (illus.).
Columbus Gallery of Fine Arts, Columbus, Ohio, *Paintings by George Bellows*, March 21–April 21, 1957, no. 18, n.p.
The Gallery of Modern Art, New York, *George Bellows, Paintings, Drawings, Lithographs*, March 15–May 1, 1966, no. 23, pp. 9, 21 (illus.).
Hirschl & Adler Galleries, New York, *George Bellows (1882–1925)*, May 1971, no. 4, n.p. (illus.).

REFERENCES

Artist's Record Book A, p. 89.

Bellows, Emma. *The Paintings of George Bellows* (New York, 1929), no. 29 (illus.), n.p.

Braider, Donald. *George Bellows and the Ashcan School of Painting* (New York, 1971), p. 67.

Esquire, 1936 (illus.).

Jewell, Edward Alden. Review of Bellows exhibition at H. V. Allison, *New York Times*, October 25, 1942.

Morgan, Charles H. *George Bellows, Painter of America* (New York, 1965), pp. 125, 127, 129, 283, 327 (illus.).

"News and Notes of the Art World." *New York Times* (magazine section), January 29, 1911, part 5, p. 15, col. 2.

Young, Mahonri S. *The Paintings of George Bellows* (New York, 1973), pp. 58, 59 (illus.).

On September 23, 1910, George Bellows married Emma Louise Story, a former art student he had met at a dance at the New York School of Art in 1904. After the wedding, the couple took a train to Montauk, on the easternmost point of Long Island, spending several days there before traveling to Sag Harbor, where Bellows introduced his bride to his parents.[1]

Shore House, a nearly square monumental depiction of the isolated beauty of Montauk, is entered in Bellows' records with the date January 1911, the first work he created that year. It was painted from a sketch Bellows made while on his honeymoon and stands as a link between Winslow Homer's Prout's Neck seascapes depicting nature's powerful forces and Edward Hopper's poignant scenes of isolated houses by the sea.[2] Bellows admitted that Winslow Homer was his "favorite pet," and the relationship of *Shore House* to Homer's work was noted as early as 1911 by a critic who reviewed Bellows' first one-man show held at New York's Madison Gallery: "Almost invariably, . . . he suggests life and force by the swiftness of his brush stroke and the elimination of non-essential forms. . . . He arrives at mastery by simple means in the 'Shore House,' a square house set on a beach with a massive blue sea beyond as gaunt and dignified in arrangement as a Winslow Homer; . . ."[3]

Executed with rich, broad brushstrokes, this rugged landscape proves that, although Bellows is known more as a figure painter and observer of urban life, he was equally adept and expressive in portraying nature. Like Homer's seascapes, the painting is a poetic scene of the natural elements: brown cliffs, light blue sky above a very high horizon line, and a dark, blue-gray ocean with green-and-white foam. Bellows' ocean continues to churn and to create rhythmic swells even on the canvas. Bellows has given us a stark, elegiac, and lonely world. There is sparse vegetation and one solitary frame house, which, although it abuts a cliff, appears frail and vulnerable, dwarfed by the vast empty space surrounding it.

Shore House is modern in its simplicity and in its large masses of color, but it is timeless in its spirituality and surely must rank as one of George Bellows' crowning achievements.

1. Donald Braider, in *George Bellows and the Ashcan School of Painting* (New York, 1971), p. 64, reports that the couple spent only their wedding night at Montauk, traveling to Sag Harbor the next day. This would have left little time for sketching. Charles H. Morgan, in *George Bellows, Painter of America* (New York, 1965), p. 120, tells us that George and Emma stayed several days at Montauk.
2. Edward Hopper studied with Robert Henri in New York at the same time as Bellows.
3. Morgan, *Painter of America*, p. 272. "News and Notes of the Art World," *New York Times* (magazine section), January 29, 1911, part 5, p. 15, col. 2.

46.
JEROME MYERS (1867–1940)

Self-Portrait, c. 1895
charcoal on paper, 12 × 9¼ in. (30.5 × 23.5 cm)
Inscribed l.r. [by the artist's wife]: "JEROME MYERS / EM"

PROVENANCE
Estate of the artist
[Kraushaar Galleries, New York]
Paul Magriel, New York, 1963

EXHIBITIONS
Finch College Museum of Art, New York, *American*

Drawings (Benjamin West to the Present) from the Paul Magriel Collection, June 9–August 31, 1961, no. 53, n.p.
The Parrish Art Museum, Southampton, New York, *American Drawings from the Paul Magriel Collection*, September 23–October 7, 1961.
Isaac Delgado Museum, New Orleans Museum of Art, *American Drawings from the Paul Magriel Collection*, November 1–December 31, 1961.

These drawings include portrait studies of individual steelworkers, their dwellings, and their labor at the hot furnaces. In an era of inhumane working conditions and labor disputes, Stella undoubtedly sympathized with the plight of the steelworkers, a large number of whom were recent immigrants like himself. In *Pittsburgh, Winter*, Stella captured the spirit of the paradoxical setting, a city of rapid economic growth yet shrouded in the oppressive smoke and soot of its major industry. Although days darkened by smog were common, Stella is not merely presenting a literal transcription of the scene. He unites sure draftsmanship with an impressionistic modulation of the overcast sky, thereby romanticizing the view.

Shortly after the Pittsburgh series was completed, Stella traveled to France and Italy. When he returned to New York several years later, many of the city images he subsequently produced express the dynamism and abstraction of the Futurist vocabulary.

48.
CHARLES DEMUTH (1883–1935)

Pepper and Tomatoes, c. 1927–1928
watercolor and graphite on paper, 10⅝ × 15⅜ in. (27.0 × 39.1 cm)

PROVENANCE
Estate of the artist
Robert Locher, 1935
Richard W. C. Weyand, Lancaster, Pennsylvania
(Sale, Parke-Bernet Galleries, New York, *Watercolors and Paintings by Charles Demuth American: 1883–1935, Part One of the Artist's Own Collection Belonging to the Estate of the late Richard W. C.Weyand, Lancaster, Pennsylvania*, October 16, 1957, no. 71)
[Babcock Galleries, New York, 1957]

EXHIBITIONS
The Brooklyn Museum, Brooklyn, New York, *American Painting: Selections from the Collection of Daniel and Rita Fraad*, June 9–September 20, 1964; Addison Gallery of American Art, Phillips Academy, Andover, Massachusetts, October 10–November 8, 1964, no. 59, p. 69 (illus.).
The Gallery of Modern Art, New York, *Major 19th and 20th Century Drawings*, January 19–February 21, 1965.
The Metropolitan Museum of Art, New York, *200 Years of Watercolor Painting in America: An Exhibition Commemorating the Centennial of the American Watercolor Society*, December 8, 1966–January 29, 1967, no. 201, p. 30.

REFERENCES
Farnham, Emily. "Charles Demuth: His Life, Psychology and Works." Ph.D. diss., Ohio State University (1959), no. 478, pp. 600–601, as *Red Pepper and Tomatoes*.
Norton, Thomas, ed. *Homage to Charles Demuth—Still Life Painter of Lancaster* (Ephrata, Penn., 1978), p. 7 (illus.).

As a student at the Pennsylvania Academy of the Fine Arts, Demuth studied under two leading art instructors of the era, Thomas Anshutz and William Merritt Chase. Two years of study in Paris, the first trip in 1904 and another made three years later, introduced him to European modernism and to the still lifes of Cézanne. The French artist's experiments with unconventional spatial arrangements exercised a profound influence on Demuth's watercolors, a medium in which he was extraordinarily proficient. Although Demuth was an active participant in New York City art circles, the artist frequently returned to

the relative seclusion of his native Lancaster, Pennsylvania, where he lived with his mother, Augusta. There, he drew upon subjects redolent of childhood memories, including local architecture, flowers gathered from his mother's garden, and the fruits and vegetables she purchased from the local farmers' markets.

The still lifes executed in the 1920s include colorful, complex arrangements of flowers and vegetables augmented by porcelain and drapery props. Increasingly, Demuth's still-life compositions focused on fewer objects. In *Pepper and Tomatoes*, delicate graphite lines combined with a modicum of brushstrokes describe the convincingly volumetric forms. United through an undulating line, the bright red tomatoes and pepper are set against a single large form, possibly an incipient eggplant, rendered in a light purple wash. Additional graphite lines located beneath and behind the objects suggest that the artist anticipated shadows and forms never fully realized.

49.

EDWARD HOPPER (1882–1967)

Houses on the Beach, Gloucester, 1923–1924
watercolor and graphite on paper, 13¾ × 19⅞ in. (34.9 × 50.5 cm)
Inscribed l.r.: "Edward Hopper"

PROVENANCE
[Rehn Gallery, New York, 1956]

EXHIBITIONS
The Brooklyn Museum, Brooklyn, New York, *American
    Painting: Selections from the Collection of Daniel and Rita
    Fraad*, June 9–September 20, 1964, no. 62, p. 73 (illus.).
Whitney Museum of American Art, New York, *Edward
    Hopper*, September 29–November 29, 1964, no. 79,
    p. 66.

REFERENCES
Kramer, Hilton. "In the Museums." *Art in America* 52, no. 2
    (April 1964): 39 (illus.).

Marking his initial venture into the medium, in 1923 Edward Hopper undertook a series of watercolors depicting the streets and houses of Gloucester, Massachusetts, one of several New England towns where he and, beginning in 1924, his wife traveled in the summer. To this time, neither Hopper's oil paintings nor his etchings, the latter which had occupied the artist from 1915 to 1923, had engendered significant public recognition. However, the Brooklyn Museum's purchase of one watercolor from the Gloucester series, *The Mansard Roof*, signaled an upturn in his career, and an exhibition at New York's Rehn Gallery followed in 1924. All of the works in this exhibition were sold, and the artist continued to be represented by the gallery for many years.

An early reference to one of Hopper's favorite themes, the structure that dominates *Houses on the Beach, Gloucester* has been isolated within the composition. Silhouetted against a nearly empty sky, the porch columns, chimneys, dormer windows, and gabled roof form an iconic image of American architecture. A bulkhead capped by a balustrade creates a horizontal barrier, further setting the house apart from its neighbor and rendering it less inviting to human habitation. Hopper employed subdued gray, blue, and green washes, which he allowed to drip, achieving a fluidity he later avoided in his more opaque watercolors.

50.

REGINALD MARSH (1898–1954)

Railroad Yard, 1929
watercolor and graphite on paper, 13¼ × 19¼ in. (33.7 × 48.9 cm)
Inscribed l.r.: "Reginald Marsh /1929"

PROVENANCE
The artist
Private collection
(Sale, Parke-Bernet Galleries, New York, *American and Ca-
    nadian Paintings and Drawings, Nineteenth and Twentieth
    Centuries*, March 14, 1968, no. 146.)
[Hirschl & Adler Galleries, New York, 1968]

As a child, Reginald Marsh played in the freight yards near his home in New Jersey, an experience which may have stimulated his lifelong fascination with the trains he recorded in his drawings, prints, and tempera paintings. The impetus to take up the locomotive as subject was recounted by the artist himself: "Begin to tire of dandyism in toto. I'll never forget a locomotive in *The Dial* by E. E. Cummings. . . . Seeing a Burchfield watercolor in the same magazine starts me doing locomotives."[1] Generally selecting an urban setting for his train images, Marsh portrayed the train as a powerful machine, devoid of a glamorous veneer. The trains are animated even at rest, either being serviced or discarded in the scrap yard. Although man is an integral element of the scenario in *Railroad Yard*, his subordinate role to the engine is clearly delineated.

The immediacy and liveliness of the drawing is a result of Marsh's early experiences as an illustrator. In 1920, following graduation from Yale, where his drawings for the campus newspaper, the *Yale Record*, earned him distinction, Marsh settled in New York City and published illustrations in the *New York Daily News* and the *New Yorker*. Marsh's monochromatic *Railroad Yard* exemplifies his flair for capturing the essentials of his subject by utilizing broad washes to create light and dark values with a wiry, descriptive line. The cylindrical mass of the emerging engine is echoed in the diagonals of the power lines and tracks, characteristic of the dynamism of Marsh's works depicting other urban subject matter.

While Marsh's trademark works were generally restricted to his New York environs—the Bowery, Coney Island, and burlesque theaters—his freight-yard scenes were frequently a result of the artist's travels throughout the United States. Another version of *Railroad Yard*'s composition, an etching entitled *Loco L.V.R.R. Locomotive Lehigh Valley* (October 13, 1929), indicates that the subject for the drawing in the Fraad collection is, too, located in eastern Pennsylvania.[2]

1. Lloyd Goodrich, *Reginald Marsh* (New York, 1972), p. 26. According to Goodrich, Marsh made this statement in 1922. However, Marsh was probably referring to illustrations that appeared somewhat later. Burchfield's *Scrapped Engines* was illustrated in *The Dial*, May 1924 (following p. 406). E. E. Cummings' wash drawing of a locomotive appeared in *The Dial*, December 1927 (following p. 500).
2. Norman Sasowsky, *The Prints of Reginald Marsh* (New York, 1976), no. 84, p. 136.

51.

CHARLES SHEELER (1883–1965)

Shaker Barns, 1945
tempera (and gouache?) on paper, 12⅜ × 19 in. (31.4 × 48.2 cm)
Inscribed l.r.: "Sheeler-1945"

PROVENANCE
[Downtown Gallery, New York]
Mrs. J. Cheever Cowdin, New York, 1945
[Davis Gallery, New York, 1962]

EXHIBITIONS
Downtown Gallery, New York, *Charles Sheeler*, 1946, no.
    15.
The Brooklyn Museum, Brooklyn, New York, *American
    Painting: Selections from the Collection of Daniel and Rita
    Fraad*, June 9–September 20, 1964; Addison Gallery of
    American Art, Phillips Academy, Andover, Massachu-
    setts, October 10–November 8, 1964, no. 63, p. 74
    (illus.).

The Precisionist painter and photographer Charles Sheeler, born in Philadelphia, trained at that city's School of Industrial Art (1900–1903) and the Pennsylvania Academy of the Fine Arts (1903–1906) under William Merritt Chase. A trip abroad with his parents in 1908 introduced Sheeler to Cézanne and analytic cubism and to the work of Piero della Francesca, whose architectonic order and design made a profound impact on the young artist.[1]

Beginning in 1910, Sheeler spent weekends near Doylestown, Pennsylvania, in rural Bucks County. He photographed the local barns, a subject that would become a favorite in his career, and studied the Shaker collection at the nearby Mercer Museum. The utilitarian design, proportion, simplicity, and durability of these objects—produced by a vanishing religious sect—held great appeal for the artist.[2] He was drawn to Shaker workmanship, characterized by the same precise and exact execution as the meticulous style that Sheeler had come to embrace in his work, whether depictions of American industry or artifacts of the Shaker folk tradition.[3]

1. Martin Friedman, Bartlett Hayes, and Charles Millard, *Charles Sheeler* (Washington, D.C., 1968), p. 11. Sheeler collected Shaker objects, which often appear in his photographs, drawings, and paintings.
2. Faith and Edward D. Andrews, "Sheeler and the Shakers," *Art in America* 53, no. 1 (February 1965): 90–95.
3. For a discussion of Sheeler and Precisionism, see Rick Stewart, "Charles Sheeler, William Carlos Williams, and Precisionism: A Redefinition," *Arts* 58, no. 3 (November 1983): 100–114.

Shaker Barns of 1945 is one of a series of paintings and drawings that combines Sheeler's interest in rural architecture and Shaker design. Although the exact buildings have not been identified, the setting is probably the Shaker colony at New Lebanon, New York.[4] The painting is a study of clear, crisp light and shadow, cool, pristine forms, and a geometrically ordered composition. The work's sharp focus reflects Sheeler's photography, as do the muted colors, which, incidentally, are also representative of Shaker aesthetics. Sheeler has given us a cropped view of an unadorned and functional building, composed of interlocking patterns of shapes and a combination of textures. Shadows play an important role, creating distinct shapes of their own across the highly finished surface of the painting, and add a disquieting quality to the work.

The world Sheeler creates is a timeless one, devoid of human participation. No figures are included in the scene, and Sheeler, with anonymous brushstrokes, has eliminated the artist's presence as well.[5] *Shaker Barns* is a permanent still life, mysterious in its emptiness and isolation.

4. Sheeler created most of his Shaker paintings at New Lebanon. I am grateful to Rick Stewart for this information.
5. Sheeler said he did not want to "see any more than is absolutely necessary of the physical materials that go into a picture" (Martin Friedman, "The Art of Charles Sheeler: Americana in a Vacuum," in Friedman, Hayes, and Millard, *Charles Sheeler*, p. 36).

INDEX

Académie Julian, Paris 24, 36, 46
Adams, John Quincy 2
Alcott, Louisa May
    Little Women 6
Alexander, John White 22
Allston, Washington 15
Altschul, Arthur xi
American Water Color Society 8, 10, 12
Anshutz, Thomas 19–21, 76, 86, 100
    Ironworkers: Noontime 20
    Two Boys by a Boat 21
    Two Boys by a Boat—Near Cape May 19–21, cat. no. 9
Armory Show 64, 72
Art Institute of Chicago 38, 64
Art Students League, New York 36, 38, 80, 86, 98, 99
Ashcan School xiii, 20, 82, 90
Augusta, Maine 3

Babcock family 10
Back Bay Station, Boston 36
Bacon, Peggy 80
Barbizon 38, 46
Barnes, Albert C., Dr. 74
Bathers (Edward Henry Potthast) 48
Beach Scene (Edward Henry Potthast) 48–49, cat. no. 22
Bellows, George 67, 70, 72, 90–96
    Forty-Two Kids 92
    Kids 90–92, cat. no. 43
    The Knock Out 92–94, cat. no. 44
    A Knockout 94
    River Rats 92
    Shore House 94–96, cat. no. 45
Bellport, Long Island 75
Belmar, New Jersey 76
Berry Picking (Eastman Johnson) 4
Between Rounds (Thomas Eakins) 92
The Black Hat (John Sloan) 80–81, cat. no. 38
Blake, William 66
Boldini, Giovanni 28
Bonnard, Pierre 52
Boston, Massachusetts 6, 36–37, 46, 52, 60
Boston Watercolor Club 58

Botticelli, Alessandro 64
Boudin, Eugène-Louis 48
The Boxing Match (William Glackens) 92
Boy Picking Apples (Winslow Homer) 8
Brittany 66
Brooklyn Museum 102
Bufford's lithography shop, Boston 2, 6
Bunker, Dennis Miller 36–37
    The Station 36–37, cat. no. 16
Byzantine mosaics 62

Cabby at the Plaza (George Luks) 88
The Cabby (George Luks) 90
The Cabby (New York Cabby) (George Luks) 86–88,
    cat. no. 41
California Pacific Exposition 68
Cape Cod School of Art, Provincetown, Massachusetts 89
Capri, Italy 56
Carolus-Duran, Emile Auguste 28
Central Park, New York 60
Century (magazine) 64, 80
Cézanne, Paul 62, 74, 100, 106
Charcoal Club, Philadelphia 80
Chase, William Merritt 20, 22, 36, 42–43, 48, 66, 88,
    100, 106
    For the Little One 26
    Landscape, Shinnecock Hills 42–43, cat. no. 19
Chez Mouquin (William Glackens) 74
Christy, Howard Chandler 74
Church, Frederic E. 15
Cincinnati Museum Association Art School 48
Cincinnati, Ohio 44, 48
Circus Band (Maurice B. Prendergast) 52–53, cat. no. 24
Civil War 6
Cole, Thomas 15
Colliers (magazine) 80, 84
Columbus, Ohio 90
Cooper Union, New York 46, 98
Coquelin, Benoît-Constant 29
Corcoran Gallery of Art, Washington, D.C. 46
Cori and the Kitten (Robert Henri) 70
Cornell, Fred 93

Cornhusking (Eastman Johnson) 4
Cos Cob, Connecticut 40–41
di Cosimo, Piero 64
Courbet, Gustave 22
Courtyard, West End Boston Library (Maurice B.
    Prendergast) 58
Courtyard West End Library, Boston (Maurice B.
    Prendergast) 58
Cowles Art School, Boston 36
Cozad, Robert Henry. *See* Henri, Robert
The Craftsman (magazine) 70
Cranberry Harvest (Eastman Johnson) 4
Cubism, analytic 106
Cullercoats, England 12
Cummings, E.E.
    The Dial 104
Cumulus Clouds, East River (Robert Henri) 66–68,
    cat. no. 31
Currier, J. Frank 22, 30
Curtis, Daniel, family 28
Curtis, Ralph 30

Daumier, Honoré 91, 94
Davies, Arthur Bowen 64–68
    Dream (or *Measure of Dreams*) 64
    Nude in Landscape 64–66, cat. no. 30
Davis, Edward 76
Davis, Stuart 67, 76, 77
Degas, Edgar 20, 26, 52, 82
Delaware River, New Jersey 20
The Delft Horse (Gari Melchers) 26
Demuth, Augusta 101
Demuth, Charles 20, 100–101
    Pepper and Tomatoes 100–101, cat. no. 48
Detroit, Michigan 24
Dewing, Thomas Wilmer 18, 64
The Dial (E.E. Cummings) 104
Dolce Far Niente (John Singer Sargent) 34
Doylestown, Pennsylvania 106
Drawbridge—Long Branch Rail Road, Near Mianus
    (Theodore Robinson) 40–41, cat. no. 18
Dream (or *Measure of Dreams*) (Arthur Bowen Davies) 64
Durand, Asher B. 15
Düsseldorf, Germany 4, 24, 86
Duveneck Boys 22
Duveneck, Frank 22–23, 44, 48
    Portrait of Emil Carlsen 22–23, cat. no. 10

Eakins, Thomas 16–18, 19–21
    Between Rounds 92
    Study for the Portrait of Miss Emily Sartain 16–18,
        cat. no. 8
East River, New York 67
Ecole des Beaux-Arts, Paris 16, 24, 36
Egmond-aan-zee, Holland 24
The Eight xiii, 19, 62, 64, 66, 70, 74, 86, 98

Emerson, Ralph Waldo 2
Eva Green (Robert Henri) 70

Fitch, Clyde 82
Five Sketches of Young Boys (Winslow Homer) 4
Flirtation Lugubre (John Singer Sargent) 28
Florence, Italy 22, 28, 56
For the Little One (William Merritt Chase) 26
Forty-Two Kids (George Bellows) 92
The Fountain at West Church, Boston (Maurice B.
    Prendergast) 58–59, cat. no. 27
Fountainbleau, France 38
The Fox Hunt (Winslow Homer) 14
Fraad, Rita and Daniel xi
della Francesca, Piero 106
Fuller, George 15
Futurists 100

Ganz, Jr., Jo Ann and Julian xi
Gardner, Isabella Stewart 30
Genre painting 4, 6, 20, 28, 30
Gibson, Charles Dana 74
Gifford, Sanford Robinson 28
Giverny, France 38, 40, 46
Glackens, William 20, 66, 72–76, 82
    The Boxing Match 92
    Chez Mouquin 74
    Untitled (Seated Woman) 72–74, cat. no. 34
    Yellow Bath House and Sailboats, Bellport, L.I. 74–76,
        cat. no. 35
Gloucester, Fishermen's Houses (John Henry Twachtman)
    44–45, cat. no. 20
Gloucester, Massachusetts 44, 102
Goldstone, Herbert xi
Goya, Francisco José de 86, 94
The Grand Canal, Venice (Maurice B. Prendergast) 54
Gray Day, Jersey Coast (John Sloan) 76–78, cat. no. 36
Green Apples (J. T. Trowbridge) 6
Green Apples (Winslow Homer) 8
Green Apples (Boy Picking Apples) (Winslow Homer) 6–8,
    cat. no. 3
Greenwich, Connecticut 40
Grez, France 38
Group of Convalescent Soldiers (John Singer Sargent) 32
Group with Parasols (A Siesta) (John Singer Sargent)
    34–36, cat. no. 15

The Hague 4
Hals, Frans 22, 29, 70, 86, 88
Harbor View Hotel (John Henry Twachtman) 44
Harper's (magazine) 84
Harper's Weekly (magazine) 6
Harrison, Leonard 34–36
Harrison, Peter 36
Harrison, Peter, Mr. and Mrs. 34
Hassam, Childe 46

Hawthorne, Charles Webster 88–90
  The Morning Coffee 88–90, cat. no. 42
Hawthorne, Joseph 90
Hawthorne, Nathaniel 2
Head of a Woman (Eastman Johnson) 2–3, cat. no. 1
Henri, Marjorie Organ 70, 72
Henri, Robert 20, 66–72, 74, 76, 82, 90
  Cori and the Kitten 70
  Cumulus Clouds, East River 66–68, cat. no. 31
  Eva Green 70
  La Neige 68
  The Sketchers in the Woods 71–72, cat. no. 33
  Sylvester—Smiling 68–70, 90, cat. no. 32
Hind, Charles Lewis 26
His Favorite Model (Theodore Robinson) 40
Hitchcock, George 24
Hitchcock, Henriette (Miggles) 24
Hogarth, William 91
Holly Beach, New Jersey 20
Homer, Winslow 2, 4, 6–14, 48, 50, 96
  Boy Picking Apples 8
  Five Sketches of Young Boys 4
  The Fox Hunt 14
  Green Apples 8
  Green Apples (Boy Picking Apples) 6–8, cat. no. 3
  Inside the Bar 12
  Porter Apples 8
  Prout's Neck in Winter 13–14, cat. no. 6
  Sand and Sky (Carrying Catch along a Beach) 11–12,
    cat. no. 5
  Spring 8–10, cat. no. 4
Hopper, Edward 67, 96, 102–103
  Houses on the Beach, Gloucester 102–103, cat. no. 49
  The Mansard Roof 102
Horowitz, Raymond and Margaret xi
Houghton Farm (Mountainville, New York) 10
Houses on the Beach, Gloucester (Edward Hopper)
    102–103, cat. no. 49

Impressionism xii–xiii, 20, 36, 38, 40, 46, 48, 72, 74
Inside the Bar (Winslow Homer) 12
Interior design 38
Italian Renaissance architecture 56
Ironworkers: Noontime (Thomas Anshutz) 20

James, Henry 30
Johnson, Eastman 2–5, 6
  Berry Picking 4
  Cornhusking 4
  Cranberry Harvest 4
  Head of a Woman 2–3, cat. no. 1
  Studies of Children 4–5, cat. no. 2

Keefe, Ed 93
Kids (George Bellows) 90–92, cat. no. 43
King, Moses 93

Klauber, Alice 68, 70
The Knock Out (George Bellows) 83, 92–94, cat. no. 44
A Knockout (George Bellows) 94

LaFarge, John 15, 38
La Jolla, California 70
Lancaster, Pennsylvania 101
Landscape (Albert Pinkham Ryder) 14–15, cat. no. 7
Landscape, Shinnecock Hills (William Merritt Chase)
    42–43, cat. no. 19
Lawson, Ernest 74
Leibl, Wilhelm 22
Lewis-Hind, Henriette 26
Lincoln Arcade, New York 93
The Little White House (Willard
    Leroy Metcalf) 46–47, cat. no. 21
Little Women (Louisa May Alcott) 6
Loch Haven, Pennsylvania 76
Loco L.V.R.R. Locomotive Lehigh Valley (Reginald
    Marsh) 104
Locomotion photography 21
London Cabby (George Luks) 88
London, England 86
Long Island, New York 36
Longfellow, Henry Wadsworth 2
Lotos Club, New York 83
Lowell, Massachusetts 46
Luks, George 66, 86–88, 90, 92
  The Cabby 90
  Cabby at the Plaza 88
  The Cabby (New York Cabby) 86–88, cat. no. 41
  London Cabby 88
  The Spielers 90
  Wrestlers 92

Macbeth Galleries, New York 41, 66
Macbeth, William 68
Madison, Dolley 2
Madison Gallery, New York 96
Mallarmé, Stephane 66
Manet, Edouard 26, 36, 74
The Mansard Roof (Edward Hopper) 102
Maratta, Hardesty 72, 78
Marblehead Rocks (Maurice B. Prendergast) 62–63,
    cat. no. 29
Marie (model for Theodore Robinson) 40
Marin, John 20
Marlowe, Julia 82
Marsh, Reginald 80, 104–105
  Loco L.V.R.R. Locomotive Lehigh Valley 104
  Railroad Yard 104–105, cat. no. 50
Marshall, William 14
Matisse, Henri 62, 74
Maurice River, New Jersey 20
McMicken School of Design, Cincinnati 48

Melchers, Gari 24–26
   The Delft Horse 26
   Portrait of Mrs. George Hitchcock 24–26, cat. no. 11
Mellor, Lilian 34–35
Metcalf, Willard Leroy 46–47
   The Little White House 46–47, cat. no. 21
Mexico City, Mexico 64
Mianus River, Connecticut 41
Milch Galleries 46
Mr. Bodley Abroad (Horace E. Scudder) 8
Modernism 62, 100
Monet, Claude 36, 40, 46
Monhegan Island, Maine 72
Monotype medium 52
Montauk, Long Island 96
Moran, Thomas 28
The Morning Coffee (Charles Webster Hawthorne) 88–90,
   cat. no. 42
Munich, Germany 22, 42, 44, 48, 86
Munich style xii, 22, 42
Muybridge, Eadweard 21
Myers, Jerome 96–98
   Self-Portrait 96–98, cat. no. 46
Mysticism 15

Nabis 62
Nantucket, Massachusetts 4
National Academy of Design, New York xiii, 8, 14, 19, 36,
   38, 66
Naturalism 20, 74
La Neige (Robert Henri) 68
New Bedford, Massachusetts 14
New Lebanon, New York 107
New York City 6, 10, 14, 42, 46, 48, 64, 66, 74, 76, 80, 82,
   86, 88, 90, 98, 99, 104
New York Daily News 104
New York Herald 84
New York Journal 84
New York School of Art 66, 90, 96, 99
New York Times 84, 86
New Yorker (magazine) 104
Newfoundland, Canada 52
Nouveau Cirque 52
Nude in Landscape (Arthur B. Davies) 64–66, cat. no. 30

Ohio State University 90
"Old Ben" (model for Charles Hawthorne) 89–90
Old Lyme, Connecticut 47
Our Young Folks (magazine) 8
Out of a Job—News of the Unemployed (Everett Shinn)
   84–85, cat. no. 40

Page, William 15
Palazzo Barbaro, Venice 28, 30
Palazzo Rezzonico, Venice 28
Palmer, Dos 34–35
Paris, France 4, 28, 66, 68, 86, 100

Pène du Bois, Guy 67
Pennsylvania Academy of the Fine Arts, Philadelphia 16,
   19, 66, 74, 76, 82, 86, 100, 106
Pepper and Tomatoes (Charles Demuth) 100–101, cat. no. 48
Philadelphia Evening Bulletin (newspaper) 86
Philadelphia Inquirer (newspaper) 76, 82
Philadelphia Ledger (newspaper) 82
Philadelphia, Pennsylvania 16, 74, 76, 82, 106
Philadelphia Press (newspaper) 76, 82, 86
Philadelphia School of Design for Women 16, 66
Photography, locomotion 21
Piazza del Campo, Siena 199
Picnicking Children—Central Park (Maurice B. Prendergast)
   60–61, cat. no. 28
The Picnic (Maurice B. Prendergast) 60
Pissarro, Camille 20
Pittsburgh, Winter (Joseph Stella) 98–100, cat. no. 47
Playfair, Hugh, Dr. 32
Plein air paintings 42
Porter Apples (Winslow Homer) 8
Portland, Maine 2
Portrait of Emil Carlsen (Frank Duveneck) 22–23, cat.
   no. 10
Portrait of Mrs. George Hitchcock (Gari Melchers) 24–26,
   cat. no. 11
Portraiture 16, 18, 22, 24, 26, 68, 70, 86, 88–90, 98
The Meyer Potamkins xi
Potter, Edna 64
Potthast, Edward Henry 48–51
   Bathers 48
   Beach Scene 48–49, cat. no. 22
   A Summer's Night 50–51, cat. no. 23
Precisionism 106
Prendergast, Charles 52
Prendergast, Maurice B. 28, 52–63
   Circus Band 52–53, cat. no. 24
   Courtyard, West End Boston Library 58
   Courtyard West End Library, Boston 58
   The Fountain at West Church, Boston 58–59, cat. no. 27
   The Grand Canal, Venice 54
   Marblehead Rocks 62–63, cat. no. 29
   Picnicking Children—Central Park 60–61, cat. no. 28
   The Picnic 60
   Siena 56–57, cat. no. 26
   Venice 54–55, cat. no. 25
   West Church, Boston 58
The Press (Philadelphia newspaper) 74
Prout's Neck in Winter (Winslow Homer) 13–14, cat. no. 6
Prout's Neck, Maine 12, 13, 96
Provincetown, Massachusetts 89
The Public Ledger (Philadelphia newspaper) 74
Puvis de Chavannes, Pierre 64

Quidor, John 15

Railroad Yard (Reginald Marsh) 104–105, cat. no. 50
Realism xii–xiii, 20, 90, 94

The Record (Philadelphia newspaper) 74
The Red Gown (His Favorite Model) (Theodore Robinson)
    38–40, cat. no. 17
Rehn Gallery, New York 102
Rembrandt (Rembrandt Harmenszoon van Rijn) 86, 98
Renoir, Auguste 20, 74, 76
Rialto Bridge, Venice 54
River Rats (George Bellows) 92
Robinson, Theodore 38–41, 46, 66
    Drawbridge—Long Branch Rail Road, Near Mianus
        40–41, cat. no. 18
    His Favorite Model 40
    The Red Gown (His Favorite Model) 38–40, cat. no. 17
    La Vachère 38
Romanticism 15, 50
Rome, Italy 28, 56
Rubens, Peter Paul 98
Ruhl, Arthur 84
"Ruth J." (model for Robert Henri) 72
Ryder, Albert Pinkham 14–15, 50, 64
    Landscape 14–15, cat. no. 7

St. Louis, Missouri 42
Sand and Sky (Carrying Catch along a Beach) (Winslow
    Homer) 11–12, cat. no. 5
Santi Apostoli, Church of 28
Santiago de Compostela, Spain 32
Sargent, John Singer 18, 26–36, 37, 72
    Dolce Far Niente 34
    Flirtation Lugubre 28
    Group of Convalescent Soldiers 32
    Group with Parasols (A Siesta) 34–36, cat. no. 15
    A Siesta 35
    A Spanish Barracks 32–33, cat. no. 14
    Spanish Soldiers 32–33
    A Street in Venice 28
    Street in Venice 28
    Studies for Venetian Street Scenes 30–31, cat. no. 13
    Sulphur Match 28
    Venetian Street 26–29, cat. no. 12
Sartain, Emily 16–18, 66
Sartain, John 16
Sartain, William 16
Schamberg, Morton Livingston 20
School of Industrial Art, Philadelphia 106
Schunemunk Mountain, New York 10
Scribner's (magazine) 84
Scudder, Horace E.
    Mr. Bodley Abroad 8
Seated Woman (William Glackens) 72–74, cat. no. 34
Self-Portrait (Jerome Myers) 96–98, cat. no. 46
Seurat, Georges 20, 52
Shaker Barns (Charles Sheeler) 106–107, cat. no. 51
Shaker design 107
Sharkey, Tom 93
Sheeler, Charles 20, 106–107
    Shaker Barns 106–107, cat. no. 51

Shinn, Everett 20, 66, 82–85
    Out of a Job—News of the Unemployed 84–85, cat. no. 40
    Stage Scene 82–83, cat. no. 39
Shinnecock, Long Island 42, 88
Shinnecock School of Art, Long Island 42
Shore House (George Bellows) 94–96, cat. no. 45
Siena, Italy 56
Siena (Maurice B. Prendergast) 56–57, cat. no. 26
A Siesta (John Singer Sargent) 35
The Sketchers in the Woods (Robert Henri) 71–72, cat. no. 33
Sloan, Dolly 76
Sloan, Helen Farr 77, 78
Sloan, John 20, 66, 76–81
    The Black Hat 80–81, cat. no. 38
    Gray Day, Jersey Coast 76–78, cat. no. 36
    Woman on Couch 78–79, 80, cat. no. 37
Smith, Francis Hopkinson 30
Society of American Artists 14, 92
Sorolla y Bastida, Joaquín 48
A Spanish Barracks (John Singer Sargent) 32–33, cat.
    no. 14
Spanish Soldiers (John Singer Sargent) 32–33
The Spielers (George Luks) 90
Spring (Winslow Homer) 8–10, cat. no. 4
Stage Scene (Everett Shinn) 82–83, cat. no. 39
The Station (Dennis Miller Bunker) 36–37, cat. no. 16
Stella, Joseph 98–100
    Pittsburgh, Winter 98–100, cat. no. 47
Still lifes 101
Story, Emma Louise 96
A Street in Venice (John Singer Sargent) 28
Street in Venice (John Singer Sargent) 28
Studies for Venetian Street Scenes (John Singer Sargent)
    30–31, cat. no. 13
Studies of Children (Eastman Johnson) 4–5, cat. no. 2
Study for the Portrait of Miss Emily Sartain (Thomas
    Eakins) 16–18, cat. no. 8
Sulphur Match (John Singer Sargent) 28
A Summer's Night (Edward Henry Potthast) 50–51, cat.
    no. 23
The Survey (magazine) 99
Sylvester—Smiling (Robert Henri) 68–70, 90, cat. no. 32
Symbolism xiii, 66

Tarbell, Edmund 36
Ten American Painters 44, 46, 48
Thayer, Abbott H. 18, 64
Tom Sharkey's Athletic Club 93
"Tommyites" 20
Toulouse-Lautrec, Henri 52, 82
Treadwell, Prentice 38
Trowbridge, J.T.
    Green Apples 8
Twachtman, John 22, 40, 44–45, 46, 66
    Gloucester, Fishermen's Houses 44–45, cat. no. 20
    Harbor View Hotel 44
Two Boys by a Boat (Thomas Anshutz) 21

Two Boys by a Boat—Near Cape May (Thomas Anshutz)
19–21, cat. no. 9

University of Pennsylvania 21
Untitled (Seated Woman) (William Glackens) 72–74, cat.
no. 34
Utica, New York 64

La Vachère (Theodore Robinson) 38
Valentine, Lawson 10
Van Gogh, Vincent 98
Vedder, Elihu 15
Velásquez, Diego Rodriguez de Silva y 29, 86
Venetian Street (John Singer Sargent) 26–29, cat. no. 12
Venice, Italy 22, 28, 30, 44, 54, 56, 66, 90
Venice (Maurice B. Prendergast) 54–55, cat. no. 25
Vermeer, Jan 26
Vermont 40
Viani, Gigia 28
Vuillard, Edouard 52

Washington, D.C. 2
Water Color Society 10
"Waverly Street Players" 82
Weir, J. Alden 40
West Church, Boston (Maurice B. Prendergast) 58
Whistler, James McNeill 15, 28, 68
Whitman, Walt 68
Williamsport, Pennsylvania 86
Woman on Couch (John Sloan) 78–79, 80, cat. no. 37
Woodstown, New Jersey 82
Wrestlers (George Luks) 92

Yale Record (newspaper) 104
Yale University 104
Yellow Bath House and Sailboats, Bellport, L.I. (William
Glackens) 74–76, cat. no. 35

PHOTOGRAPHIC CREDITS

Archives of American Art, fig. 1
Oliver Baker Associates, cat. no. 40
Brenwasser, cat. nos. 31, 43
Geoffrey Clements, cat. nos. 10, 47
Cleveland Museum of Art, fig. 3
Helga Photo Studio, cat. nos. 4, 9, 11, 12, 15, 17, 18, 20,
21, 23, 24, 25, 26, 27, 28, 29, 32, 35, 36, 39, 41, 45, 50
Sean Purtell, cat. no. 13
Nathan Rabin, cat. no. 16
Walter Rosenblum, cat. nos. 1, 2, 3, 5, 6, 7, 10, 14, 19, 22,
30, 34, 37, 38, 42, 46, 48, 49, 51
Sotheby's, New York, fig. 2
Studio/Nine, Inc., cat. no. 44